SOUTHERN
BOOK PUBLISHERS

GORILLAS

Photography and text by Karl Ammann
Introduction by Richard Leakey
Edited by Francis Dorai
Design Direction by V. Barl
Directed by Hans Höfer

INSIGHT TOPICS

Insight Topic
Gorillas
© **1997 Apa Publications (HK) Ltd**
Photography and text by Karl Ammann
Design Direction by V. Barl
Concept by Hans Höfer
Edited by Francis Dorai
First Edition
ISBN 9-62421-189-2

All Rights Reserved
Manufactured in Singapore
by Höfer Press Pte. Ltd.

First South African edition, 1997
Published by Southern Book Publishers (Pty) Ltd.
PO Box 3103, Halfway House, 1685, South Africa
ISBN 1 86812 695 1

Contents

Foreword	21
Gorillas	23
The Mountain Gorilla	31
Battle of the Giants	77
The Eastern Lowland Gorilla	85
The Western Lowland Gorilla	131
Saving the Great Apes	151
Conservation Recommendations	161

The Virunga volcanoes as seen from Rwanda. Gahinga (3,474m/11,380ft) in the centre, is flanked by Sabyinyo

(3,534m/11,595ft) on the left, and Muhabura (4,127m/13,540ft) on the right. Clear days like this in the Virungas are rare.

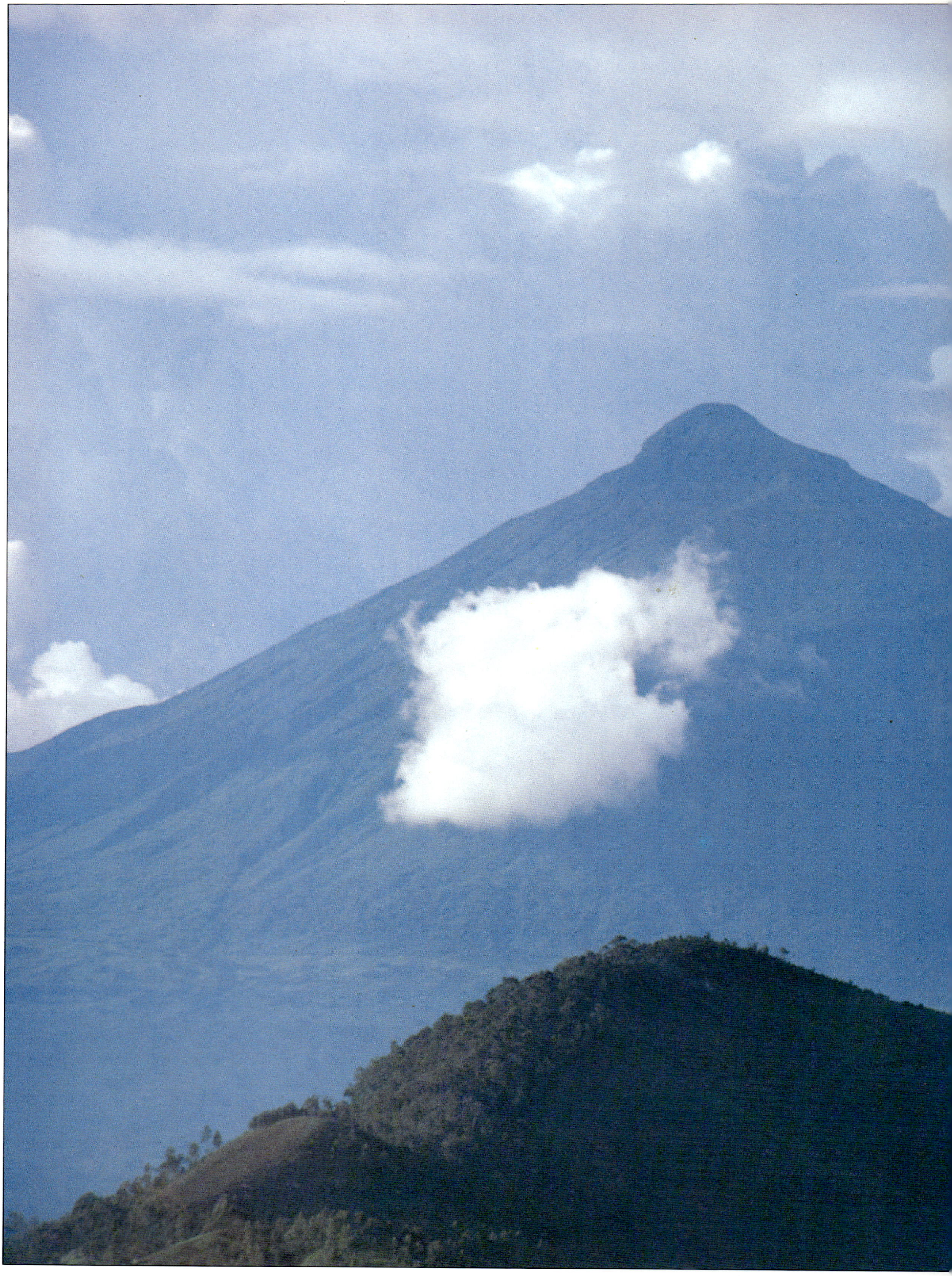

Mahabura, the tallest of the three peaks (4,127m/13,540ft), photographed from Djomba, Zaire.

Before the tribal unrest of 1994, Rwanda was the most densely populated country in Africa.

Every available hillside was used for cultivation.

Mahabura and Gahinga as seen from the Zairian side.

Despite familiarity with tourists, villagers sometimes still consider their cameras intrusive.

Some years ago, land was excised from the Virunga National Park in Rwanda for the villagers

to plant a cash crop, pyrethrum, used in the manufacture of insecticides. Prices later collapsed.

14

A riot of colours at Djomba's weekly Thursday market.

16

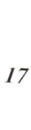

A street supermarket in the North Kivu province.

The mountain gorilla's habitat covers the montane forest of the Virunga range bordering Rwanda and Zaire to Uganda.

Morning often starts with mist obscuring the sunrise.

Portrait of Rugabo, a silverback mountain gorilla, who features extensively in this book

Foreword

Gorillas and chimpanzees are our closest relatives and although they are placed in a separate "family" from humans, we share much in common. Indeed, many eminent scientists have long recommended that apes be re-classified and included in the same family as humans and our fossil ancestors. I, for one, would certainly support such a move. Perhaps only then would people show more concern for our simian relatives, their rights and their future.

Our record is not impressive when it comes to taking care of the remaining great apes of Africa. Forests are being cleared for timber and agriculture at an alarming rate, which in turn allows hunters and poachers to penetrate deeper into virgin territory in search of animals which can be sold for their meat. In recent years, bush meat, which refers to any kind of game meat from antelope to gorilla, has become one of the main sources of protein in Central and West Africa. As a result, both subspecies of lowland gorillas, along with chimpanzees and bonobos are threatened with extinction. Gorillas are especially vulnerable to these hunters as, apart from being a source of meat, their body parts are used in local fetishes and black magic.

In the case of the mountain gorilla, however, loss of habitat is the major threat to their existence. In terms of sheer numbers, the mountain gorilla is the most vulnerable of the three subspecies as there are only a few hundred individuals left. The countries where mountain gorillas are found, Rwanda, Zaire and the western edge of Uganda, are poor and troubled with hundreds of thousands of people living under deplorable circumstances. Civil wars have displaced people from the cities and suburban towns. Left to fend for themselves as refugees, they see the forests as cheap and free hunting grounds for wood, building materials and food. In the scheme of things, it is not difficult to understand why humanitarian relief agencies are aimed at human refugees and the problems they face. But it is tragic that more thought is not given to the location of these refugee camps and their debilitating consequences on the environment.

I hope that an awareness of the plight of the gorillas may lead to more responsible action by governments and international relief agencies. In the final analysis, short-term, crisis-based responses that impact negatively on a country carry significant repercussions, a cost that is eventually borne by another group. It is far better to plan things with greater foresight, so that, in the long run, both human refugees and gorillas are given the chance of a better life. After all, whether man or beast, we all are bound by an intricate web of existence and interdependence in this increasingly tenuous world.

This book has the rare distinction of being the first and only book in the world to document all three subspecies of gorillas – the mountain, eastern lowland, and western lowland. These animals, once feared but known today to be some of the gentlest creatures on earth, have been intensively studied; and thanks to the dedication of scientists and other researchers, we now know quite a lot about gorillas. The images in the pages that follow bring out much of this intimate knowledge about these animals and how they live. There are superb pictures of young animals, old animals, happy ones, and sad ones too. There are also gruesome reminders of how man exploits the apes for meat, fetishes and skulls. The photographs provide such an evocative account of these primates that little narrative is really needed.

I am sure that this book will be a source of vicarious pleasure to many who may never have the chance to experience the gorillas on their land and on their terms. Only public concern and awareness will help put an end to the mindless slaughter of these creatures and the ever-increasing threat to their natural habitat. To that end, this informative pictorial, put together by Karl Ammann, is a superb vehicle for getting the message across.

Richard E. Leakey

Gorillas

Sport-hunter and gorilla, circa 1865

Throughout history, myth and legend have surrounded the gorilla, the largest of the great apes which live in the thick forests of Central and West Africa. There they remained, virtually unknown to the Western world until 1847, when they were discovered by Dr. Thomas Savage, an American missionary who had written a complete description of the chimpanzee in the early 1840s. Savage found a gorilla skull in a fellow missionary's home on the Gabon River and realized he'd stumbled on something important.

The discovery of the gorilla had a big impact on the public in general, and scientists in particular. Here was an unknown "monster" which the scientific community accepted as a new species. For a long time after, gorillas were seen as violent and aggressive creatures, striking out at humans at the slightest provocation. Even early scientists, like the British anatomist Richard Owen, held such notions of gorillas. In 1859, he warned of gorillas attacking humans by hoisting them up into trees and strangling them. Such exaggerated descriptions fed the public's perceptions of gorillas and reinforced their fears, fuelled in turn by popular fiction and movies of the time which depicted gorillas as chest-thumping man-eaters. Nothing could be further from the truth; in fact gorillas are shy by nature, attacking only when provoked. The discovery of the gorilla also gave rise to the question "am I ape or man?", echoing Darwin's theory of evolution and inciting fierce theological and philosophical debates on the nature of man. Today, the gorilla still ranks, for most people, as the most fascinating of the great apes. Unfortunately, the future of the last remaining great apes is threatened; civil wars and deforestation, poaching for meat and the sale of young gorillas as pets, and the use of gorilla body parts as fetishes and souvenirs all add up to a dim future for these animals.

Gorillas were once thought to be man-eating monsters

When the first gorilla was discovered in 1847, the mystery animal was regarded as a new species of the chimpanzee. It was only in 1852 that *Gorilla* was recognised as a separate genus. In the years between 1900 and 1920, taxonomists, who used arbitrary, and sometimes conflicting standards, classified more than a dozen subspecies, or races, of the *Gorilla*. Much of the confusion, however, has been dispelled, and today only three subspecies of *Gorilla* are recognised: the mountain gorilla (*G.g. berengei*), found in the Virunga volcanoes region that divides Zaire from Rwanda and Uganda; the western lowland gorilla (*G.g. gorilla*), prevalent in the lowland rainforest areas of Cameroon, Central African Republic, Gabon, Equatorial Guinea, Nigeria and the Cabinda region of Angola; and the eastern lowland gorilla (*G.g. graueri*), which lives in the lowlands and mountain forest areas of eastern Zaire. Recent genetic studies carried out at Harvard University, however, show striking differences between the DNA of the western lowland gorilla and that of the mountain and eastern lowland subspecies, lending credence to a new

Western lowland gorilla – candidate for a completely new species?

theory that the western lowland gorilla should be classified as a separate species altogether.

GORILLA BEHAVIOUR

In 1959, the eminent conservationist and scientist George Schaller, then a graduate student at the University of Wisconsin, arrived with his professor, Dr. John T. Emien, at Kabara Meadows in Zaire, between Mt. Mikeno and Karishimbi, to study the mountain gorilla. Schaller stayed for 18 months and successfully established most of the criteria for gorilla research in the wilds. As a student of animal behaviour, Schaller assumed correctly that many of the accounts concerning the ferocious nature of the greatest of the apes were exaggerated. He believed that these animals were essentially shy and would avoid confrontational encounters if possible. Schaller's initial contacts with different gorilla families confirmed this hypothesis: he tried to keep his presence as non-threatening as possible and while the animals were initially disturbed when approached by humans, the charges and displays of outrage by the male adult silverback gradually became less and less frequent. In time, some families tolerated close encounters with humans. Schaller's research was followed up by Dian Fossey's marathon in-depth observation which she started in 1967. Her project later enabled students to pursue their own studies by habituating different gorilla groups to human presence. In the Kahuzi Biega region of Zaire, Adrian Deschryver, another eminent conservationist, carried out a similar project involving a group of eastern lowland gorillas in 1965.

Social interaction during the siesta

Trackers at Kahuzi Biega collecting gorilla hair samples from a night nest for research

In 1986, I was fortunate to accompany the British naturalist Mike Catsis who successfully habituated two of the mountain gorilla groups on the Zairian side of the Virunga region, the National Park of Virunga. One of the two groups, headed by an adult silverback called Rugabo, was already considered safe for tourist visitation; with the exception of the occasional charge by the silverback, most of the gorilla family members tolerated visitors at close range.

One day, while we were starting to get ready for the trek back to camp after a visit, Rugabo approached one of the cleared pathways which facilitate access to the different parts of a group's territory. Sensing that he was not intending to charge, we all crouched in an instinctive submissive position. Catsis was in front and I was just behind him. Rugabo was standing there on all fours, his head level with that of Catsis. He stepped within inches of Catsis' face and stared intently at him, straight in the eye. Turning away momentarily as if inspecting some leaves, Rugabo returned to the eyeball to eyeball stance. Catsis was wary about what was going to happen but decided to play along. Without warning, Rugabo lifted one of his hands of the ground, touched Catsis' shoulder, pulled back, and then raised his fingers to his nose to smell them. Catsis was ecstatic: this was the first time that he had physical contact with a silverback – and one initiated by a gorilla! (*see bottom right picture on page 67*). Three years later, I witnessed a violent dispute between Rugabo and another silverback, Rugendo, for control of territory in the same area. In that primeval show of strength between the two

A gorilla youngster reaching out to a park ranger

The gorilla does not have to travel very far within its territory for food

magnificent apes, marked by terrifying screams, chest- and ground-beating, I came literally within an arm's length of the showdown (*see story and pictures pages 74–81*). Tragically, Rugabo and several others were gunned down in August 1995 in the Virunga forests, probably shot by Hutu militiamen or poachers from nearby refugee camps.

The gorilla is a lazy wanderer; it loves to rest and sunbathe between bouts of feeding. Behaviour such as chest-beating, ground-thumping, tearing of vegetation and even grooming are rare. Photographing gorillas, therefore, can be a challenging task. In different areas, gorillas feed selectively on a variety of plants, developing different eating habits. Unlike chimpanzees, gorillas do not "follow the food" since throughout most of the year there is the same amount of foliage to be had almost everywhere within the range. While the chimpanzee searches for fruit trees, the gorilla eats mostly plant stems, vines and leaves within its territory. The exception is the mountain gorilla, and some groups of eastern lowland gorilla, who move into bamboo forests when shoots are in season.

Gorillas live in fairly stable groups, each occupying its own territory, with the average covering some 20 to 30 sq km (8 to 12 sq miles), although territories may sometimes overlap. In the Virunga region between Rwanda and Uganda, the average group size is estimated to be 17, although groups of as few as two and as many as 30 have been observed. On average, a gorilla family comprises one mature silverback male, one young adult silverback male (in some cases, adult silverbacks have been found to live together peacefully in the same group), one blackback male, three adult females, and between two and three young. The dominant silverback male, recognised by his silvery grey saddle, is the focal point of a gorilla family and responsible for the group; it is the silverback who stays behind in times of danger, roars at intruders, and if need be, charges and defends the family. When hunters or poachers invade gorilla territory and encounter a gorilla family, it is generally the silverback who perishes first. The silverback does not leave the group unless he loses a fight to another silverback male from a different group, or if a young male group member develops into a silverback. The size of a group and its success in maintaining a territory seems closely linked to a silverback's prowess as a leader. Usually, group changes are due to the coming or going of adult male gorillas or the absorption of females from a group which has lost its silverback.

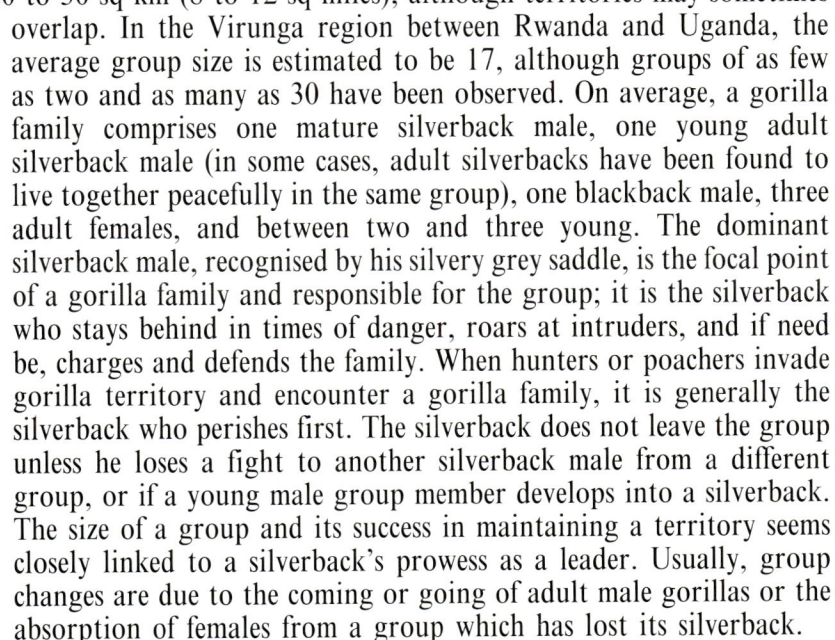

Mushamuka is believed to be the largest habituated silverback

The story of Mushamuka, an eastern lowland male, describes what happens when a silverback loses his mandate to lead. One of the oldest known silverbacks in Zaire, Mushamuka was habituated by Adrian Deschryver in 1970. Between 1980 and 1983, he became moody and difficult, and had to be taken off the "tourist circuit". He was re-habituated between 1983 and 1986 and at the time, his group consisted of 32 animals. When we visited him in February 1992, Mushamuka had just lost two more females in a fight with his son Mubalala, who controlled an adjacent territory. He was still suffering from nasty bite wounds on his hand and his head, and a gash in his lower lip resulted in a constant dribble of saliva down his chin. His group size was down to 18 and it was obvious that at an estimated age of 41, Mushamuka was past his prime and had to give way to his sons who were establishing themselves in adjacent territories.

Over 300 mountain gorillas inhabit the Virunga region

Personal Involvement

My own involvement with gorillas and gorilla tourism started in 1983 when I visited several of the habituated groups of mountain gorillas in Rwanda. Gorilla tourism had become one of the country's main sources of foreign exchange earnings and the demand for permits to view the apes often outstripped their supply. I had to book my visit several months in advance to be ensured of four consecutive days with each of the different families.

Poverty greatly hinders conservation

Encountering the greatest of the apes in its natural habitat turned out to be the experience I had expected it to be. I was, however, disappointed by the commercialism which already surrounded gorilla tourism in Rwanda. The gorilla experience ended at the park headquarters where tourists scrambled back into their mini buses for the ride back to hotels in Ruhengeri and Gisenyi. In addition, the rangers accompanying us made it clear that the viewing time would be restricted to one hour. But, they pointed out, given the right kind of incentive they had the power to extend the time period. At that time gorilla tourism was just taking off, but even then the local people had found enterprising ways of making money from tourists. Every morning on our way from the hotel in Ruhengeri to the Virunga National Park gate, we would encounter a villager in tattered clothing. He would stand in the middle of the road, a big rock in his hand, threatening to smash our windscreen unless our driver handed over a few bills. I'm sure the man was quite harmless, although our driver didn't share my optimism.

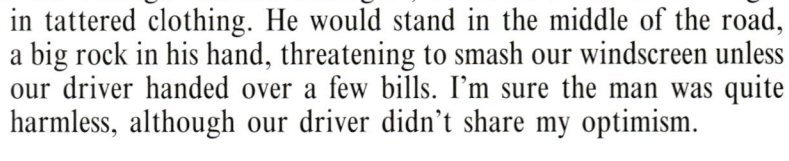

Zairian rainforest shrouded in early-morning mist

I did not return to Rwanda till 1986. By that time the situation had become much worse. In order to obtain a permit during peak season, visitors were required to book one week's accommodation in the country. On one occasion, three of us had booked and paid for eight permits (the maximum tourist group size) to ensure a more private visit. In the end two more visitors were forced on us; they had paid for their permits and we received no compensation for the two permits which now had been paid for twice. The cost of a permit in 1986 was US$100 each. In 1995, it went up to US$128, but with tourism in a deep funk because of the civil war between the Hutus and the Tutsis, United Nations and foreign aid workers are the only "tourists" today. We had asked to depart as early as possible to take advantage of the favourable morning light and clear skies. However, the rangers did not consider this sufficient reason to change their routine and we were kept waiting until 9.30am when all the other visitors belonging to different groups had arrived. After walking for over two hours we reached the gorilla groups at around midday with the sky over the Virunga laden with heavy cloud cover. During previous visits heavy rain provided a sombre backdrop for gorilla viewing and this was precisely what we wanted to avoid.

An eastern lowland silverback

It was during that visit that I heard of two groups of mountain gorillas being habituated across the border at Djomba in Zaire. Eager to find out more, I arrived in Djomba and met Mike Catsis of the Frankfurt Zoological Society, which organised and founded the habituation process of the Zairian mountain gorillas. The society had built a very basic cabin which offered shelter at the edge of the forest, just outside the park boundary. The two gorilla families were still being habituated and only a limited number of tourists were accepted on the daily excursions. To our great joy, the experience was all we had hoped for with none of the frustrations we had encountered earlier in Rwanda.

The good experience at Djomba filled my head with ideas; having just opened a luxury tented camp in Kenya's Maasai Mara reserve, I had visions of doing something similar here. On my return to Goma, the capital of Zaire's Kivu province, I sat down with a local tour operator and outlined a concept on how to present an ecologically-sensitive gorilla-viewing programme for tourists. We agreed to look for additional partners and build an environment-friendly log cabin camp near the Djomba park

The camp at Djomba

gate. Back in Nairobi, I prepared a feasibility study and presented it to two big Kenya-based tour operators. We registered a company, and ended up doing a lot more pioneering work than we had ever bargained for.

Zaire did not, and still does not have any kind of tourism infrastructure for the up-market clientele we were proposing to fly in by charter aircraft from Nairobi. Eventually we had to do everything ourselves, from hiring staff to cutting the grass on the Rutshuru airstrip – the one closest to the Djomba camp – to printing immigration forms for the officials at Goma airport. The village chiefs had to be convinced that it was worth contributing labour to maintain the road to Djomba, which after heavy rains was often impassable. Communication with the outside world was maintained via a short wave radio in an old DC3 parked at the Goma airport. However, the gorilla experience made up for it. Tourists were willing to overlook some of the shortcomings once they met the two silverbacks, the late Rugabo (whom I first met on an earlier visit in 1986), Rugendo, and their families. The gorilla families regularly came to the forest edge a few feet from the cabins and watched the construction work with curiosity. The camp, when it was finally completed in 1988, came close to what we had originally envisaged.

Mission airstrip near Djomba

However, our enthusiasm was considerably dampened when a horrendous accident occurred soon after the camp was opened: a charter aircraft crashed into the Virunga volcanoes killing all 14 of our clients on board. In addition, we were still fighting government bureaucracy to ensure that our company would receive a guaranteed number of viewing permits for both groups of gorillas at Djomba. As it stood, we were competing for a limited number of permits with tourists arriving overland to Djomba. We promised up-front payments for all permits booked, which would have amounted to 100 percent occupancy of the Djomba gorillas, hoping that further groups would then be habituated. Members of the conservation community opposed such an arrangement because they considered it a monopoly situation.

Dian Fossey, a pioneer of gorilla research and a champion of the mountain gorilla cause, had also been opposed to tourism in the initial stages, although she later realised that limited tourism was probably the most effective way to preserved the mountain gorilla and its habitat. The tourism industry in neighbouring Rwanda, which was based on the four groups of habituated gorillas, later became the third largest source of foreign exchange earnings for this tiny nation, and probably the main reason for keeping the park intact. We wanted to bring some of that revenue to Zaire and demonstrate to the Zairian authorities the benefits of carefully controlled tourism.

Watching gorillas can be therapeutic

The problems we were encountering meant that I had to travel regularly to Zaire to function as trouble-shooter. Although disappointed at the lack of progress, visiting Rugabo and Rugendo had a calming effect on me and made up for many of my frustrations. At the same time I managed to convince the rangers that

The ideal group size for gorilla viewing is six people

visitors should start the day early and that stays of 1½–2 hours with the group should be the norm rather than the exception. Group size was kept to six tourists, which in the dense vegetation, turned out to be the ideal number. For a while, we came close to being able to offer what I considered the perfect gorilla experience. By 1989, however, we started to accept the reality of doing business in Zaire: as soon as one seemingly unsurmountable problem was solved, another would arise. Maintaining standards became increasingly difficult and in the end one partner, the largest tour operator in East Africa, decided to pull out. We had no choice but to throw in the towel as well. Organising gorilla excursions of an acceptable standard took up too much of everybody's time, and problems beyond our control ate into our profit margins. Sadly, another third-world pioneering business had run its course.

PHOTOGRAPHING THE GORILLAS

I was already a keen photographer when I visited Rwanda and the mountain gorillas for the first time in 1983. In the years thereafter I published two photo book titles, taking what had started out as a hobby to a different plane altogether. My first crop of gorilla pictures were more than disappointing. Like other dedicated photographers I learnt the very hard way how difficult a photographic subject the gorilla can be. The light in the forest is often extremely poor and the dark faces and coats of the subject

Taking a gorilla by surprise can result in a mock charge

provide for very little contrast. When the sun occasionally does break through, it "burns out" the parts of skin or fur which reflect light. Natural light photography is difficult at the best of times, and using fill-in flash – at Kahuzi Biega in Zaire, the only place where it is permitted – often creates an artificial feel. I was fortunate in that my regular journeys to Zaire allowed me to work on a trial and error basis over a substantial period of time. When the photographs didn't work out, I would evaluate the material shot and refine my equipment list, film type, exposure settings and so on for the next journey. Nonetheless, even today, I still produce more material that ends up in the waste-paper basket from a gorilla excursion than any other.

In the 1980s, several coffee table-type books featuring the mountain gorilla appeared on the market. I bought them all and tried to objectively compare my picture material with what was printed, some of them by top notch professional wildlife photographers. While each title, as well as my own arbitrary selection of photographs, featured some outstanding portrait pictures and general material covering scenery and people, I found very few good shots depicting the behaviour of the great apes. The reason was simple: few professional photographers could afford to invest the time and money (between US$100–$140 a day for the permit alone) necessary to photograph gorillas over a prolonged period of time. Only a scientist studying gorillas, who has the luxury of time and free access to the gorilla viewing areas, could possibly hope to shoot a comprehensive pictorial coverage of these apes. Unfortunately, very few of the able behavioural scientists studying the gorillas today are good photographers.

Close-ups require longer lenses and higher film speeds

Over the years, I expanded the selection of my gorilla material by covering the habituated eastern lowland gorilla groups of the Kahuzi Biega, making it possible to compare this subspecies with its mountain cousin. Then, in the early 1990s, I started working on an editorial feature on the bush meat trade which resulted in regular trips to different parts of West Africa. (The results of my work on the bush meat trade and its threat to Africa's endangered species, including gorillas, are graphically illustrated in the closing chapter of this book.)

A western lowland gorilla orphan at the Brazzaville sanctuary

Photographing the western lowland subspecies was a different matter altogether. There are no habituated western lowland gorilla groups and the few glimpses I had of this subspecies when pursuing them in Gabon made it obvious that photographing them in the same way as permitted by their eastern cousins was not an option.

However, while working on the bush meat feature I kept finding baby gorillas for sale in village markets. On one of my trips I came across a female baby gorilla of the western lowland subspecies. She was lying on the dirt floor of a hut, curled up into a tight ball. The owner explained that he had brought her home three weeks ago for his children to play with after he had shot her mother for meat. Tied to a post to prevent escape, she was now lethargic and in severe distress, caused by the friction wounds around her hips. I paid US$8 for her – roughly the value of fresh gorilla meat – and delivered her to the then new gorilla sanctuary in Brazzaville, Congo Republic. While settling her in, I was allowed to accompany the adolescent group on their daily outings to a patch of forest near the orphanage. I was able to successfully shoot the missing third chapter of this book – the western lowland gorilla – making this the only photographic portfolio covering all three subspecies.

The author with a teenage sanctuary gorilla

My original plans were to combine my gorilla photographs with the ones I had taken over the years of the chimpanzee and the orangutan into a single book entitled the Great Apes. I was still working on this project when I met Hans Höfer, the noted publisher of *Insight Guides* and an old friend whom I had worked with previously on several guide books and an *Insight Topic* photobook on the Maasai Mara Game Reserve in Kenya. I mentioned my plans for the Great Apes book and his immediate reaction was: "I want to do a Topic book on the gorilla!"

I explained the limitations of my coverage and my belief that no single photographer could hope to do justice to such a challenging subject. I even tried to convince him that my orangutan coverage was far superior and that as a Singapore-based publisher, the Asian orangutan should be a creature closer to his heart. But the gorilla was what he wanted, which says something about the myth which surrounds this ape. I put my Great Ape project on hold and arranged a selection of pictures which I forwarded for his consideration. On the following pages you will find the final selection, celebrating the majestic beauty of the gorilla – mountain, eastern and western lowland.

Karl Ammann
Nanyuki, Kenya
1996

Stem-peeling is a favourite feeding technique of the mountain and eastern lowland gorilla.

The Mountain Gorilla

There are only about 340 mountain gorillas (*G.g. berengei*) in the world today, surviving in the isolated habitat of the Virunga volcanoes region, which straddles Zaire, Rwanda and Uganda – although scientists are still arguing whether the Bwindi gorillas in Uganda should belong to the mountain or the lowland subspecies. The mountain gorilla is perhaps the best known of the three gorilla subspecies, being the first to be habituated to human presence and the subject of countless books, films and documentaries. It is also regarded as the most endangered of the three subspecies because of its small numbers and low rate of reproduction.

The most easily recognizable of the three subspecies, the mountain gorilla has a noticeably longer pelage (coat) and a very broad face, with relatively narrow nostril lines and massive jaws and teeth. The males are thicker set than the western lowland gorilla, weighing, on average, about 160kg (352lbs). The females, with an average weight of 85kg (187lbs), are larger than those of the two lowland species. Mountain gorillas are the hairiest of the three subspecies and adult males are sometimes bearded for good reason: they live at altitudes of between 2,133m (7,000ft) and 3,962m (13,000ft) where temperatures can fall to below freezing point at night. In addition, fatty deposits on the top of the mountain gorilla's head also help protect the ape against the cold conditions of the mountains. It has also been claimed that the mountain gorilla's wider nasal cavity and broad chest allows for a higher oxygen intake in the thin mountain air and helps it to breathe more efficiently. The animal's basic colour is black, which makes the silvery grey saddle of the adult male a striking contrast. This black pigmentation is useful in two ways: first, it helps to attract and trap heat in the high altitudes of the mountains, and second, since mountain gorillas love to sunbathe, the pigmentation makes them less susceptible to heat stroke. Combined with its long and shaggy hair, it is obvious that these characteristics of the mountain gorilla subspecies are eminently suited to high altitude living.

The diet of the mountain gorilla consists largely of foliage. At Rwanda's Virunga National Park, studies have shown that the mountain subspecies consumes 58 different plants, of which leaves, shoots and stems account for about 86 percent of its diet; fruits and small insects making up the rest. Because foliage comprises such a great portion of their diet, feeding on insects and snails is always a learning experience for mountain gorillas, especially the young. In one amusing incident, I photographed a bout of ant eating by a group of mountain gorillas. One of the youngish males had discovered a hole in the ground swarming with large red ants. He hesitated only for a moment, stuck his hand in, grabbed a fistful and ran some distance away where he started feeding, using his lips to pluck ants from between his hairy arms and simultaneously performing some dance steps in an effort to shake off those that were biting him. Soon, several of his family members came in on the act. They would rush to the ant nest, reach into the hole and grab a handful and retreat. The gorillas had obviously learnt that lingering around the nest made them an easy target for these biting insects.

The gorillas featured in this chapter have been gravely affected by the 1994 Rwandan civil war. The former base camp for gorilla tourism on the Zairian side of the park has been taken over by refugees and the surrounding forest which the gorillas inhabit is rapidly being depleted of its resources. In addition, eight mountain gorillas have been killed so far, three of whom were shot at point blank range, including Rugabo, a majestic creature whose images appear in the following pages.

Rugendo, one of the silverback leaders of a mountain gorilla group in Zaire's Virunga National Park,

chewing on a stem that can't be too nutritious.

Meticulously picking each leaf from the stem is a leisurely experience for the gorilla. The mountain gorilla has a choice of

any of 58 types of plants in the montane forests surrounding the Virungas.

When tourists come upon a group of habituated gorillas, the initial response is one of mild curiosity.

This, however, soon gives way to the main business at hand: eating.

With feeding being one of the major activities,

finding a more artistic photographic angle can be an interesting challenge.

Feeding behaviour seems to be largely learnt rather than instinctive.

Watching mother and other group members will allow a youngster to make the appropriate decisions.

The majestic silverback Rugabo during his mid-morning siesta.

Here, he provides one of his offspring with a convenient back rest.

Top: A group of youngsters playing 'Tarzan' with the lianas.

Bottom: Watching the proceedings from behind the safety of the foliage.

Top: This youngster from the Rugendo family is still too young to play unsupervised.

Bottom: Taking cover behind Rugendo while the silverback has a closer look at the tourists.

Youngsters are usually the more curious ones. They seek a closer vantage point, and even occasionally initiate contact.

Bottom: Chest beating is a sign of discomfort. It is hard to catch this on film as the action rarely lasts longer than seconds.

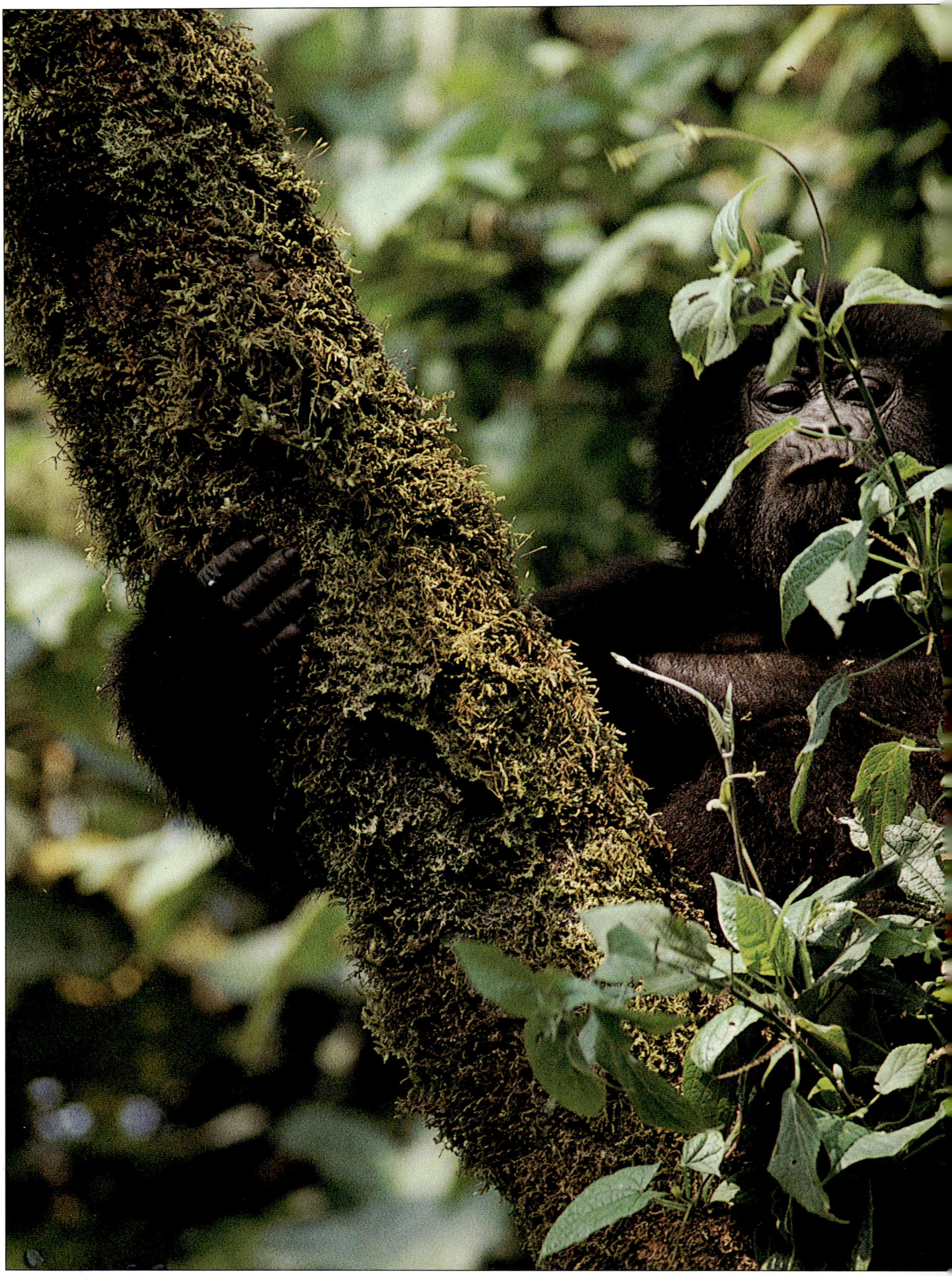

A playful youngster shows off from its perch in a hegenia tree.

While the silverback keeps an eye on things,

the rest of the family gets on with the daily tasks such as feeding, grooming or just plain dozing.

Mother and young in an apprehensive mood.

Silverback in a pose that humans can easily relate to.

Mountain gorillas live at altitudes of 2,133m (7,000ft) and 3,962m (13,000ft). In addition to the thick fur that helps to keep

them warm, fatty deposits at the top of the head also help protect the subspecies against the cold conditions.

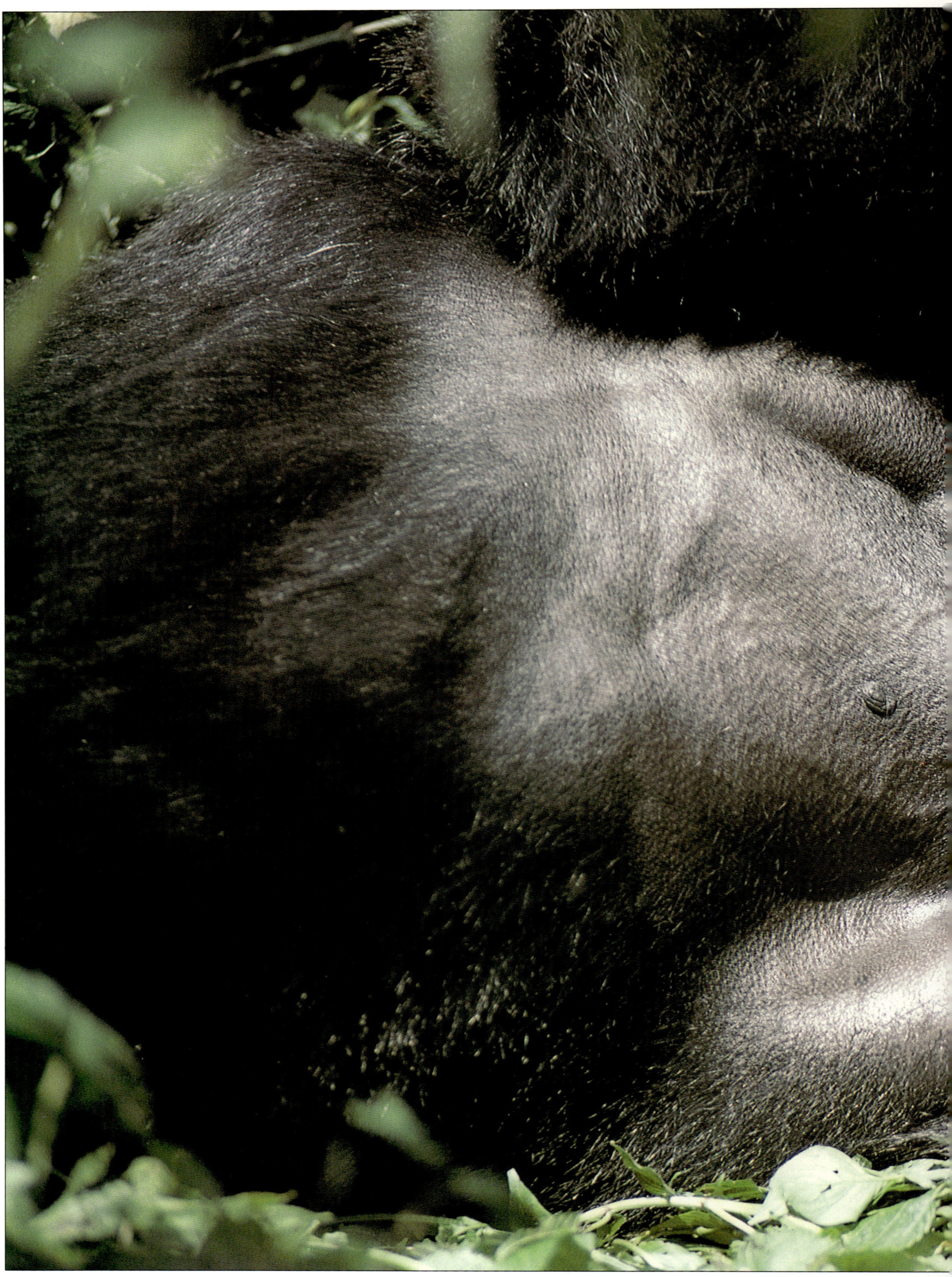

Because of the cold, gorillas love to sunbathe. Resting on a leafy bed, the sun's warmth is gratefully absorbed.

A silverback averages 160kg (352lb) in weight. As the leader of the group, he decides on where and when to forage, rest

and sleep. He also defends the family against the challenges from the other males and the worst predator – humans.

Adult males start life with sharp canines that deteriorate with age. The teeth are adapted for a fibrous diet, mainly

leaves, shoots and stems. They also occasionally eat fruit, snails, ants and grubs.

*Coming face to face with a silverback charge and smelling his breath at close range is a daunting experience.
However, more often than not it's just a bluff, abandoned at the very last moment.*

Such mock charges have mistakenly lead to gorillas being shot.

A charge by a young blackback male, angry at an outsider's intrusion into his private space.

Bottom: The photographer's defiant last picture of the blackback before he abandons the shoot.

Top: Every visitor's ambition: a photo of their encounter with a silverback. Bottom: When the gorilla family moves they prefer to use trails instead of bashing through virgin forest. Here, a ranger stands clear.

Top: A close inspection – by Rugabo – of Mike Catsis, who habituated the group to human contact.

Bottom: In a rare encounter, this youngster grabs a handful of the author's hair.

The hesitant meeting of not-too-distant relatives. Rangers find it difficult to control gorilla behaviour, particularly their own initiation of physical contact. Such contact should not be actively encouraged, because of the risk of transmission of disease.

Grooming is important bonding behaviour and helps establish the hierarchy of the group.

Females, although they may be habituated to human presence, take longer to accept outsiders.

This one prefers to stay in the background, peeking through the foliage.

Rugabo, in a reflective mood. On 13 August 1995, Rugabo, perhaps the best known

No one knows for sure the motive for the killing. Local authorities suspect of the habituated mountain gorillas, was found dead, shot twice in the chest.

Hutu militia from the surrounding refugee camps to be the culprits.

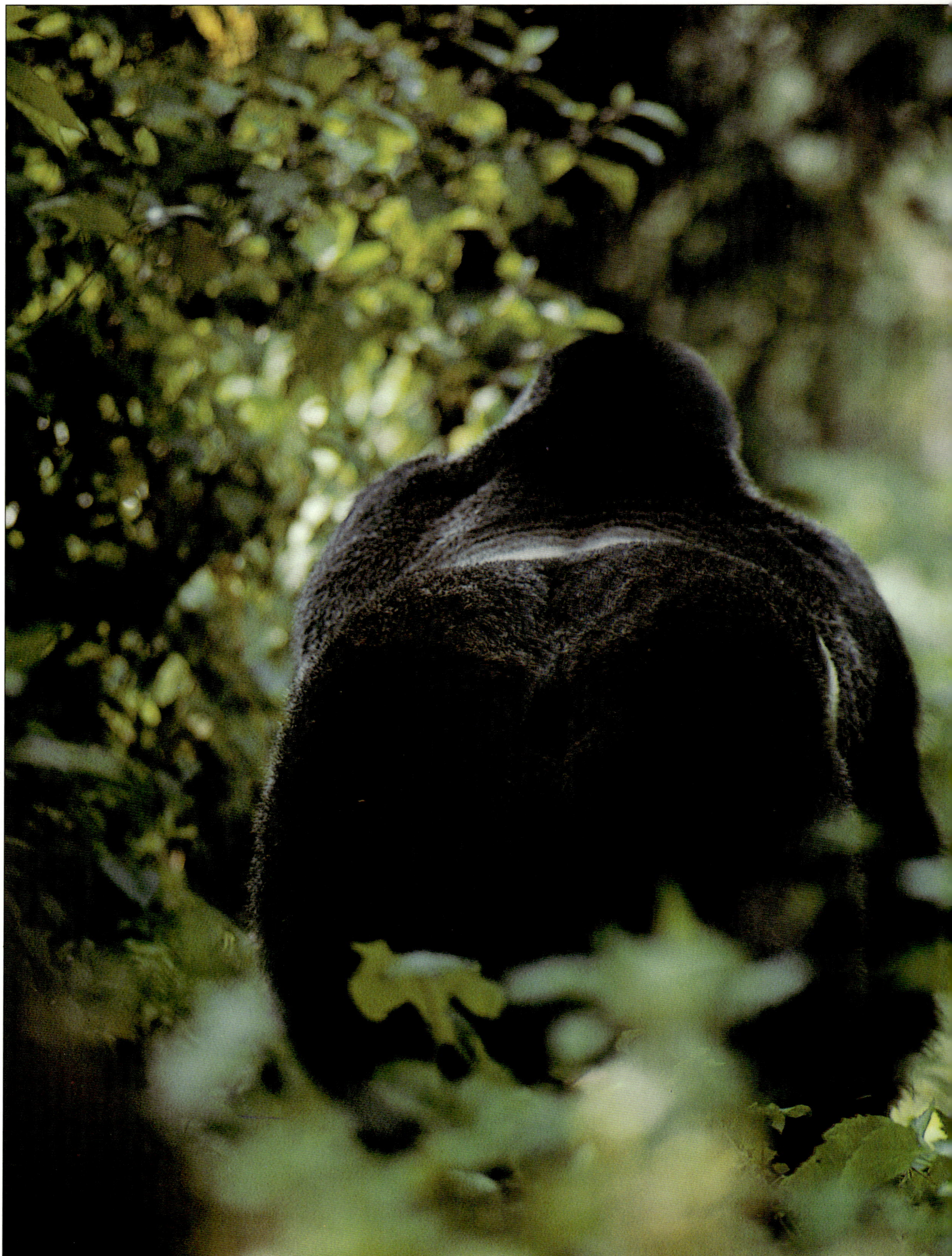

Rugabo shows off his silvery saddle while moving down a viewing trail.

Rugabo awaits Rugendo's return for round two of their battle to commence.

Battle of the Giants

In 1989, I was fortunate to witness a dispute between two silverbacks for control of territory. Seeing two huge silverback mountain gorillas taking each other on in this primeval show of strength is a memory forever etched on my mind. The following description was first published in the "East African Wildlife Society Magazine".

Accompanied by a park ranger, we left to visit the Rugabo family, one of the two groups of habituated mountain gorillas near Djomba, on the edge of Zaire's Virunga National Park. The silhouette of Mount Sabinio, the volcano closest to the camp, was barely visible under an ominously overcast morning sky. After about 30 minutes, we found fresh tracks leading off one of the paths into thick jungle. The paths, which in some places almost tunnel through the dense vegetation, allow visitors easy access to the gorilla range. We followed Rugabo's tracks behind the ranger who, with his machete, tried to clear the vegetation. After 20 minutes, the tracks led back to the path, only to suddenly disappear into the thick vegetation again. Soon, the ranger sensed the reason for Rugabo's mysterious behaviour: he was trying to confront Rugendo, the other silverback who lived with his group in territory which partially overlapped that of Rugabo's. Previous tourist groups had been aware of two similar confrontations during the past two months and it seemed that a possible territorial feud might be intensifying. Witnesses had brought back tales of terrifying screams, and chest- and ground-beating.

We were now back on the path and there, some 20 metres to the side, a youngster was hanging on the limb of a tree, looking down on the daily lot of intruders. As we moved deeper into the vegetation, we saw two of Rugabo's females sitting, their arms crossed nervously over their chests. As I peered into the thick foliage behind them, I chanced upon the arm of a silverback. As thick as a man's waist, it reached up and broke off a smallish tree with a slight movement of its wrist. Motioning us to be quiet, the ranger cleared a path with his machete, keeping an eye on the spot where we had spotted the silverback. Keeping track of the silverback's whereabouts is one of the elementary rules of gorilla watching. It allows the ranger to position himself between the tourists and the silverback in case of a gorilla charge. However, in this possible silverback confrontation, the rules had not yet been written, and it was the guide's decision as to how close an approach was safe.

Pushing forward, we came across a gorilla-made clearing. In the centre stood Rugabo, having trampled down most of the vegetation around him, while Rugendo sat on the opposite edge of the arena. This was going to be a photographer's dream except for the light, or rather the lack of it; it was 9.30am, the sky was still grey and the forest canopy allowed little light to pass through. Without warning, the action started. Rugendo made a rush through the clearing past Rugabo and raised himself on his hind legs, grabbing a handful of lianas and tearing its branches. Rugabo followed this move by changing his position, standing with hands and feet on the ground, head held high, back arched and his behind in the air – a posture I had not seen before. Slowly, he advanced on Rugendo, who stood at the other edge of the clearing. Rugabo rose on his hind legs and beating his chest, grabbed a small tree and broke it like a twig. In response, Rugendo retaliated by rushing past his adversary again and pounding the ground so that we could literally feel it vibrate. Over the next 30 minutes, this sequence of events repeated itself, with both gorillas making machismo demonstrations of their strength.

Meanwhile, the females on the side sat quietly, observing and still appearing nervous. Then, one of the youngsters rolled on his back and clapped his hands. We all broke out into laughter, defusing some of the tension in the air. Suddenly Rugendo retreated, leaving the edge of the clearing and making his way through heavy undergrowth. Rugabo followed in hot pursuit with us trampling through the forest only metres behind. But we soon lost sight of the combatants; only the crashing vegetation indicating the direction the gorillas were moving. Then, suddenly, we heard heavy crashing sounds just in front of us, followed by a piercing silverback charge scream, a terrifying sound which once heard is never forgotten. In a few seconds, we heard the sickening sound of flesh being torn; somehow we knew that this was no mere chest-beating. The ranger in front took two steps behind in retreat, stepping on my toes and causing me to fall backwards over the lady behind me and prompting a further chain reaction behind her. Picking up ourselves and our wits, we continued along the track. The undergrowth was still heavy and except for a few of Rugendo's females rushing past us to catch up with their leader, we saw no sign of the two males. The ranger was certain the show wasn't over yet.

The path had now narrowed to about a metre in width, flanked by dense wall-like vegetation. In the middle were Rugabo and Rugendo, poised for another confrontation. If we were caught in the fracas now, there would be no escape. Rugabo stood his ground, beating his chest but Rugendo kept advancing. Suddenly, the former started to retreat, and in our direction! Barely had we flattened ourselves against the vegetation when the gorillas rushed past us, less than arm's length away, giving us a good nose-full of their odours. Rugendo stood up on his hind legs and tore down a few more branches. Having shown Rugabo, and us, that he was no coward, Rugendo rushed past us again, with Rugabo hot on his heels. This sequence was repeated not once but four times. On the fourth run, Rugabo stopped and positioned himself about a metre away from us almost flattened tourists, with Rugendo opposite him. We all tried to sink back into the undergrowth as far as possible, barely breathing. Rugendo reached out, broke off a branch several inches above my head and threw it on the path. Having erected his barrier, thus signifying that the battle was over, Rugendo moved off in search of his females, leaving Rugabo standing in the middle of the path.

The encounter between the two silverbacks: Rugendo puts on a terrific display of strength,

flattening the vegetation around him, while Rugabo stands his ground.

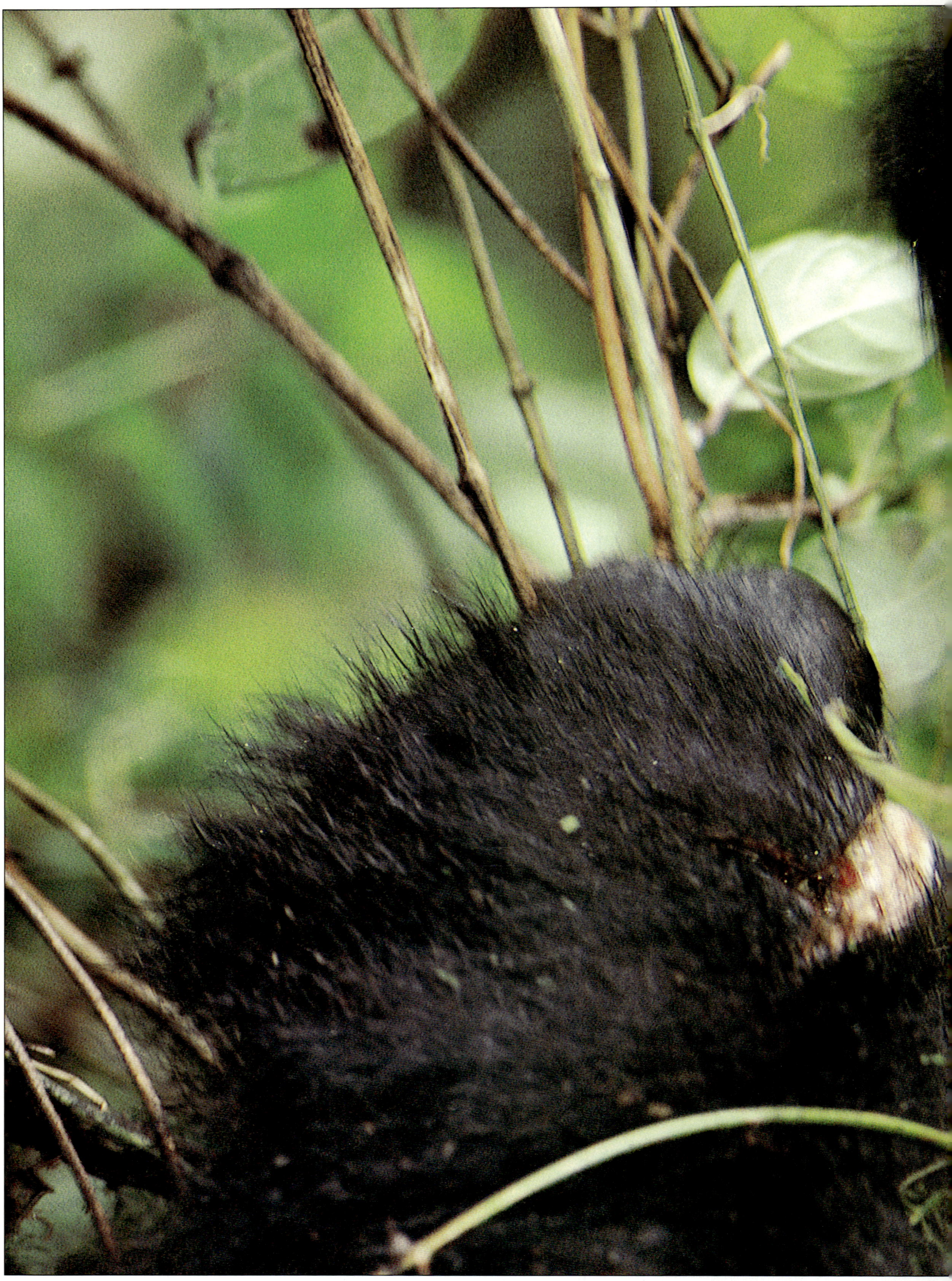

Serious injuries can sometimes result when rival silverbacks clash. Within the group, violent social interactions are rare.

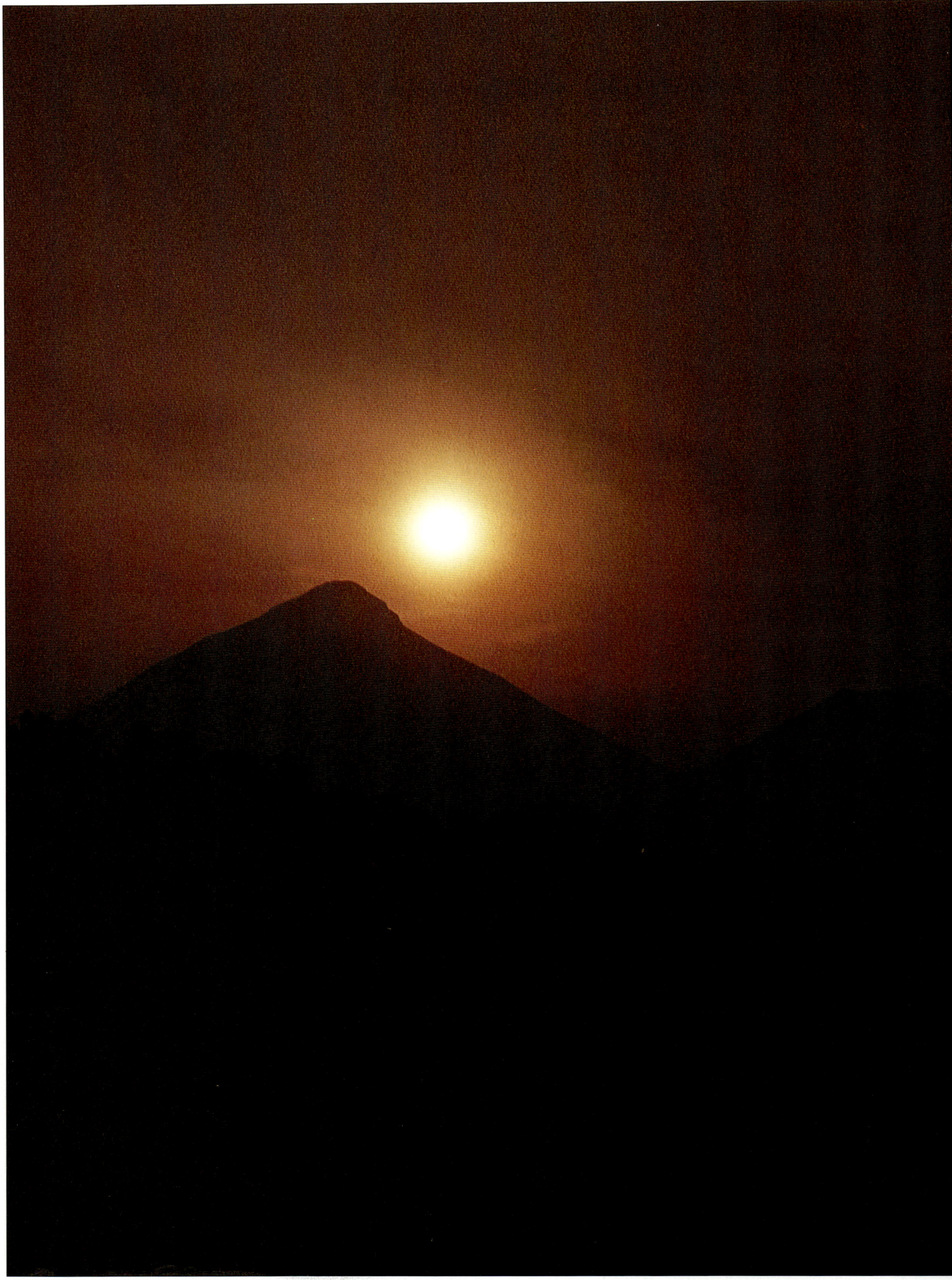

Dusk falls on Mahabura and Gahinga. This sunset view was taken from the Djomba camp in Zaire.

Fill-in flash doing its trick.

The Eastern Lowland Gorilla

The eastern lowland gorilla (*G.g. graueri*) is an intermediate race, living in the lowlands and mountain forests of eastern Zaire. There are currently some 3–5,000 of this, the physically largest of the subspecies, in existence. According to studies done by the scientist George Schaller, eastern lowland gorillas are found within a large area which stretches for about 322km (200 miles) from east to west and 482km (300 miles) from north to south in the eastern Zaire region. Within this area, the animals are found in about 60 isolated forest areas. Census figures from the Kahuzi Biega region, just northwest of Lake Kivu, show this area to have the highest concentration of eastern lowland gorillas; with a maximum of 5,000 animals spread out from the bamboo forests of the Kahuzi and Biega mountains down to the lowland forests near the headwaters of the Oso and Lugulu rivers. New research has revealed some uncertainty regarding the classification of the gorillas of the Kahuzi Biega region; although they have been traditionally lumped together with the eastern lowland gorilla, they live at an altitude similar to that of their mountain cousins across Lake Kivu. But at the same time, geographically, Kahuzi Biega is separated from the habitat of the mountain subspecies in the Virunga volcanoes region by one arm of the Great Rift Valley.

On average, the male of the eastern lowland subspecies is about 175cm (5ft 7½in) tall and weighs 165kg (364lbs). In addition, it has the advantage of having the same long arms as the western lowland gorilla and longer legs than the mountain gorilla, making it the largest of the three. Its fur is longer than that of the western lowland gorilla, but less shaggy than that of its cousin, the mountain subspecies. Both the fur and skin colour of the eastern lowland gorilla is black but rarely does it reach the intensity of the mountain gorilla. The silvery grey saddle of the male adult only covers the back unlike that of the mountain gorilla species, which extends as far down as the rump.

The face of the eastern lowland gorilla is longer and narrower than that of the mountain gorilla, but its jaws and teeth are larger and its chest broader than the western lowland gorilla. There are not enough skulls available to be certain how the gorillas of Kahuzi Biega should be classified. Living at altitudes comparable to those of its mountain cousins across Lake Kivu, they are certainly not lowland gorillas. However in geographic terms, one arm of the Great Rift Valley separates them from the mountain subspecies. Their present range is continuous from the high altitude bamboo forest of Mts. Kahuzi and Biega down to the lowland forests near the headwaters of the Oso and Lugulu rivers.

In general, the eastern gorilla is intermediate in structure between the other two subspecies. In contrast to the mountain gorilla, whose diet largely consists of foliage, it thrives on a diet of half foliage and half fruit. Invertebrates, especially ants and termites, are also eaten by lowland gorillas. The eastern lowland gorilla will leave its night nest to defecate beyond the rim, whereas the colder night temperatures up in the Virungas are perhaps the reason why the mountain gorilla has not adopted this habit and instead chooses to defecate in his nest. Gorillas are generally understood not to like water. However, in several parts of West Africa, hunters have reported seeing gorillas happily crossing rivers that are shallow enough to wade through. At Kahuzi Biega I have occasionally seen eastern lowland gorillas entering a swamp, sometimes knee-deep in water (*see pages 106–107*) to consume the reed grass that grows therein.

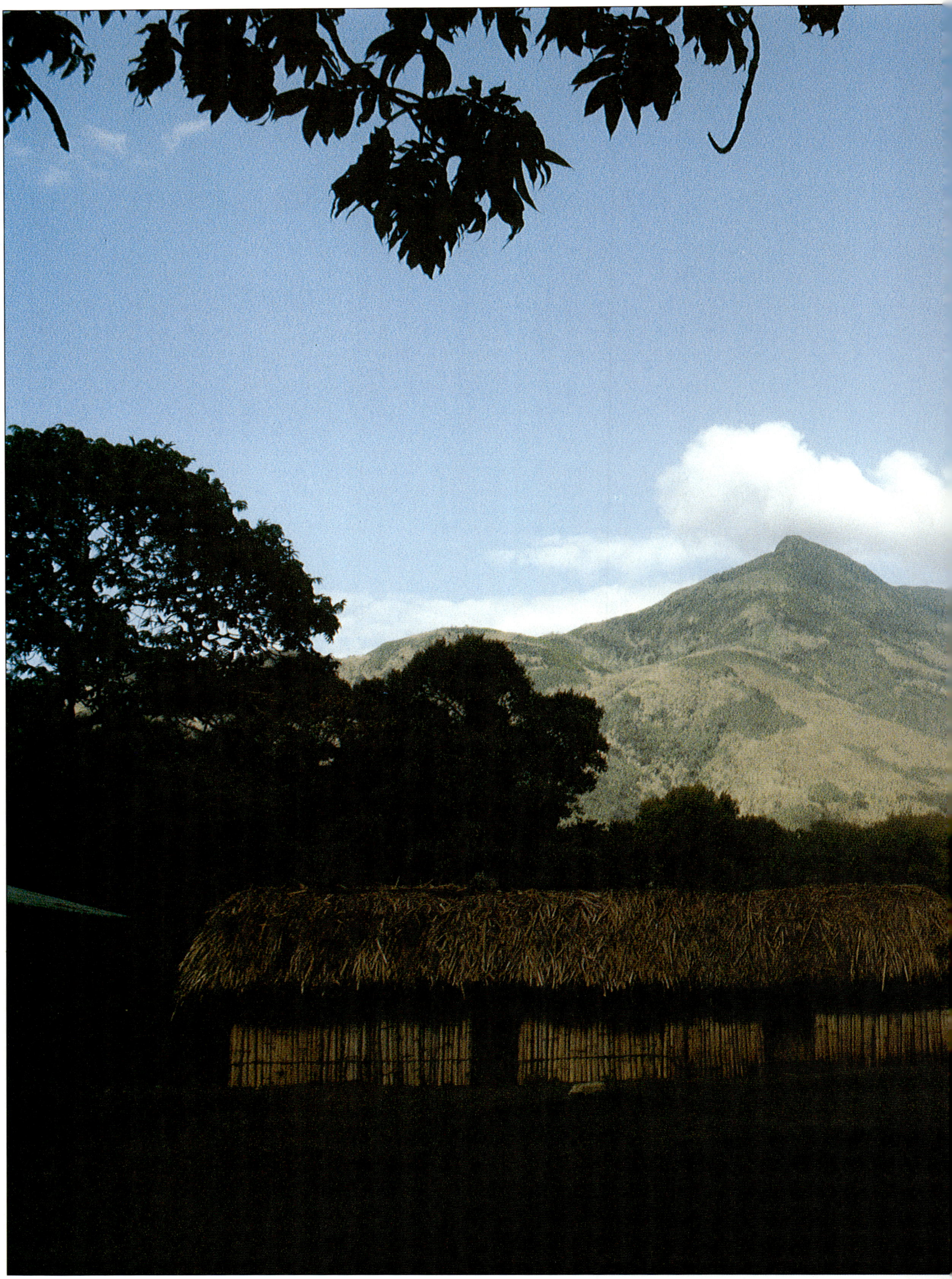

Mt. Kahuzi viewed from the western park entry gate.

The Rusizi river represents the border between Rwanda and Burundi. It also runs along the access road from

Bujumbura to eastern Zaire and the gorillas. On one of these islands lives Burundi's last elephant.

Commercial logging is not yet an issue in the forests of eastern Zaire.

However, firewood collected by the Hutu refugees has had a considerable environmental impact.

This group of 'pygmoids' – pygmies who have intermixed with the local Bantu tribe –

demonstrate the traditional art of hunting. Outside of the reserves and parks there is little game left.

94

In some parts of Zaire, foreign visitors are still a novel sight.

The montane parts of the Kahuzi Biega forest are composed of over 25 varieties of trees,

many of which are over 30m (98ft) tall and provide the perfect props for climbing.

While the youngsters of Kahuzi Biega gorilla groups are equally curious as their cousins

across the lake in the Virungas, they do not generally initiate physical contact.

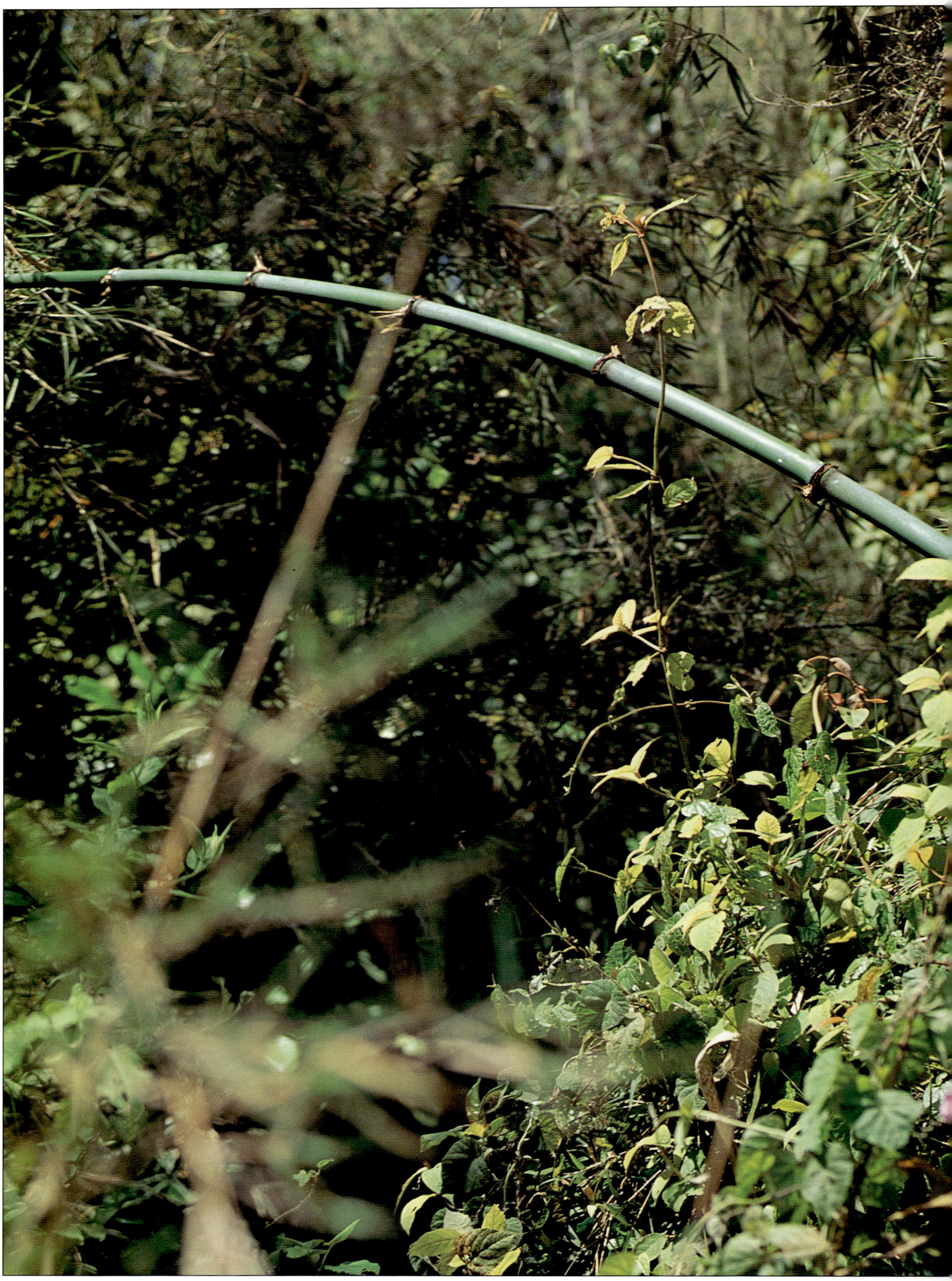

A youngster testing the elasticity of a bamboo pole.

Naninja, one of the silverback leaders of the four habituated gorilla groups, in his domain.

The gorilla diet is so rich in succulent plants and stems that they rarely need to drink water.

Two classic portraits of Naninja. The light was good enough to use slow speed film, resulting in rich, saturated colours.

105

Generally, all three subspecies of gorillas tend to avoid water. However, two of the Kahuzi Biega groups seem to be an exception, sharing territory which contains a swamp.

They wade into the swamp, feeding on the tender base of the reed grass which they pull out of the water.

Only a few days old. Masasi's latest offspring clings to its mother.

Maheshe, the father, on guard over the new addition to his family.

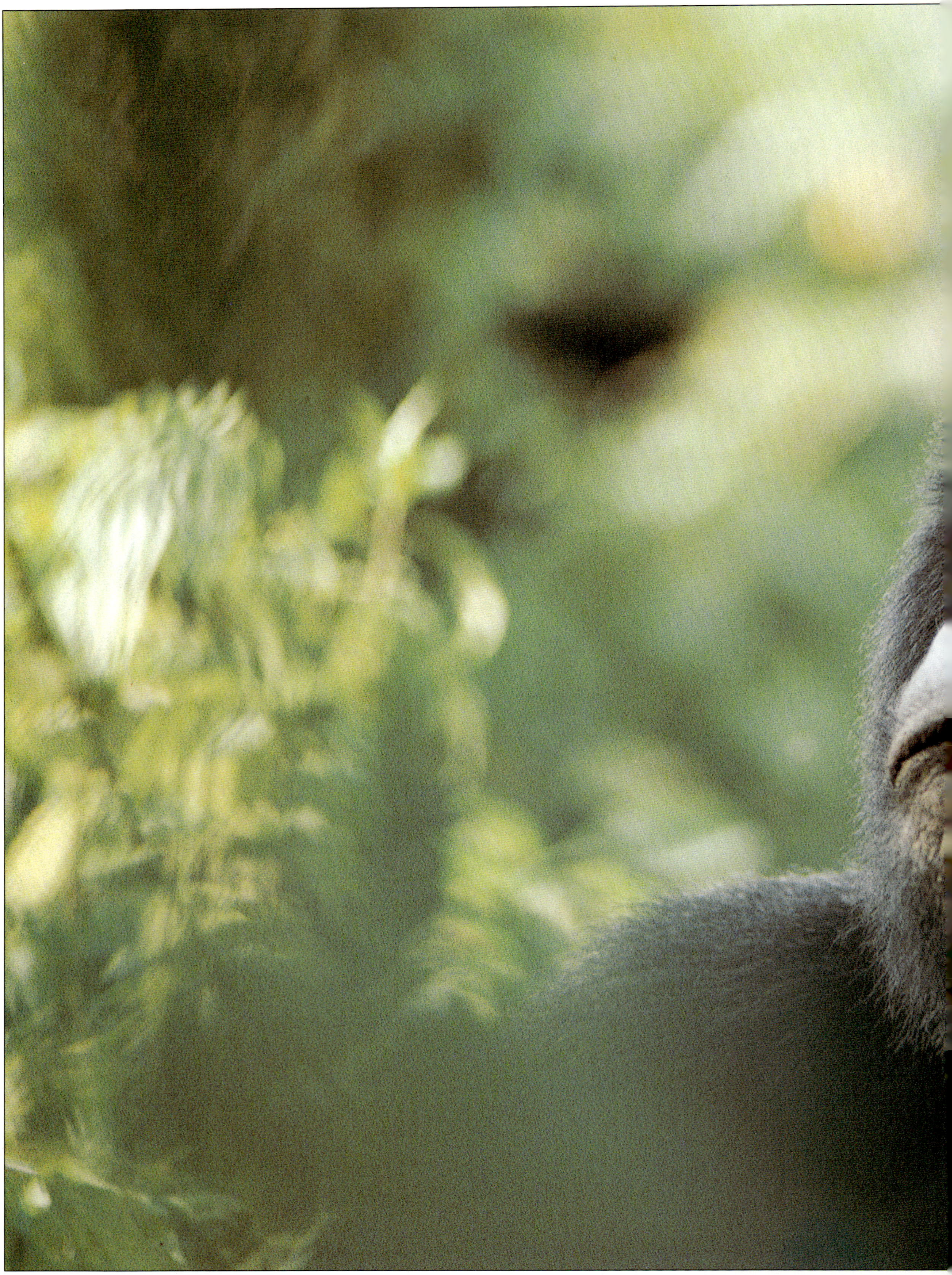

A female from Maheshe's group, keeping an eye on her tree-climbing youngster.

112

Peeking from behind the foliage, this youngster is probably wondering if it's safe to come out.

The Kahuzi Biega is so rich in vegetation that the gorillas seldom have to travel far in search of food.

Besides foliage and juicy stems, tree bark is one of the main sources of food.

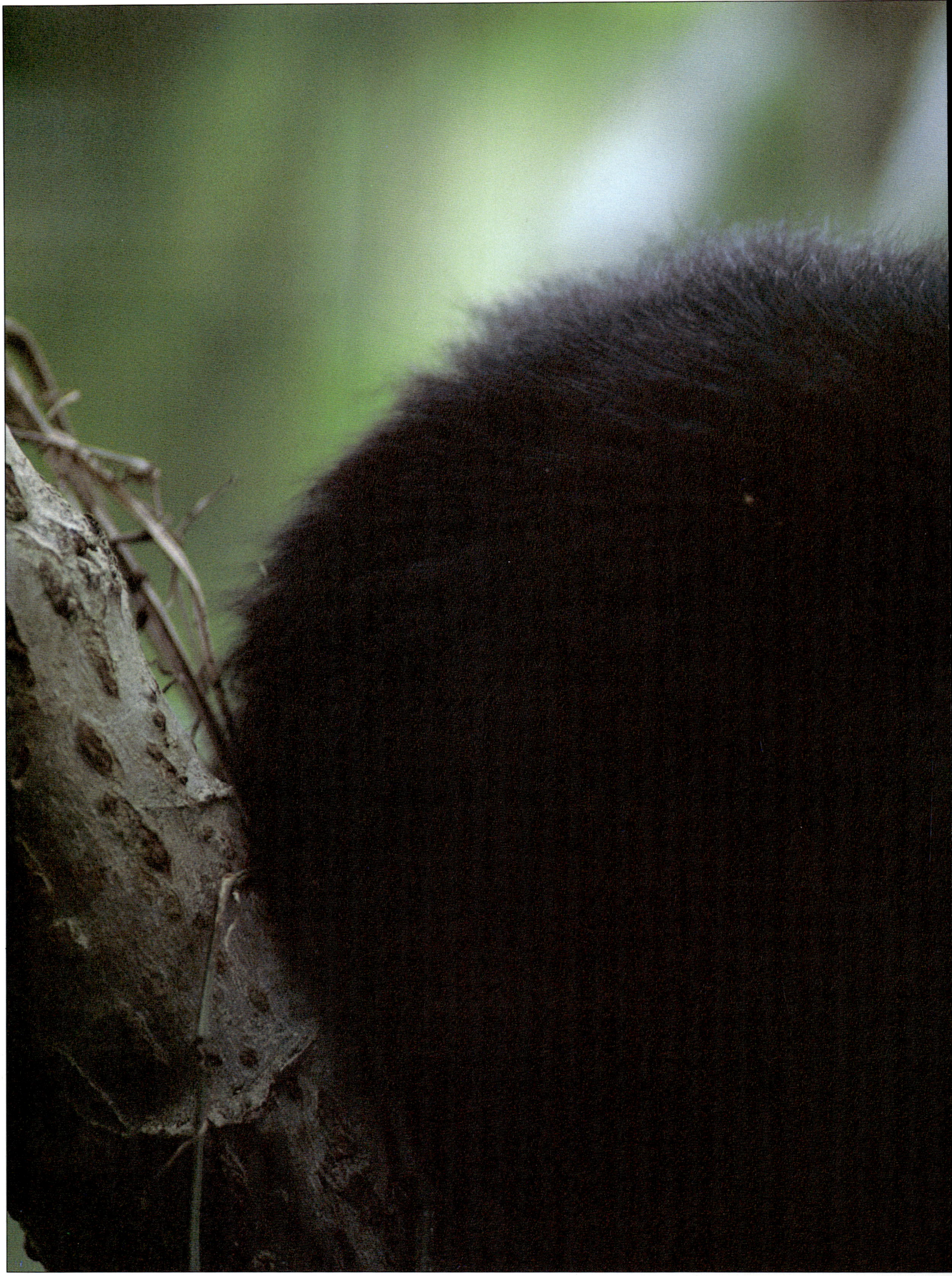

The eyes say it all. Getting some reflection in the eyes is essential to making a gorilla picture communicate to the viewer.

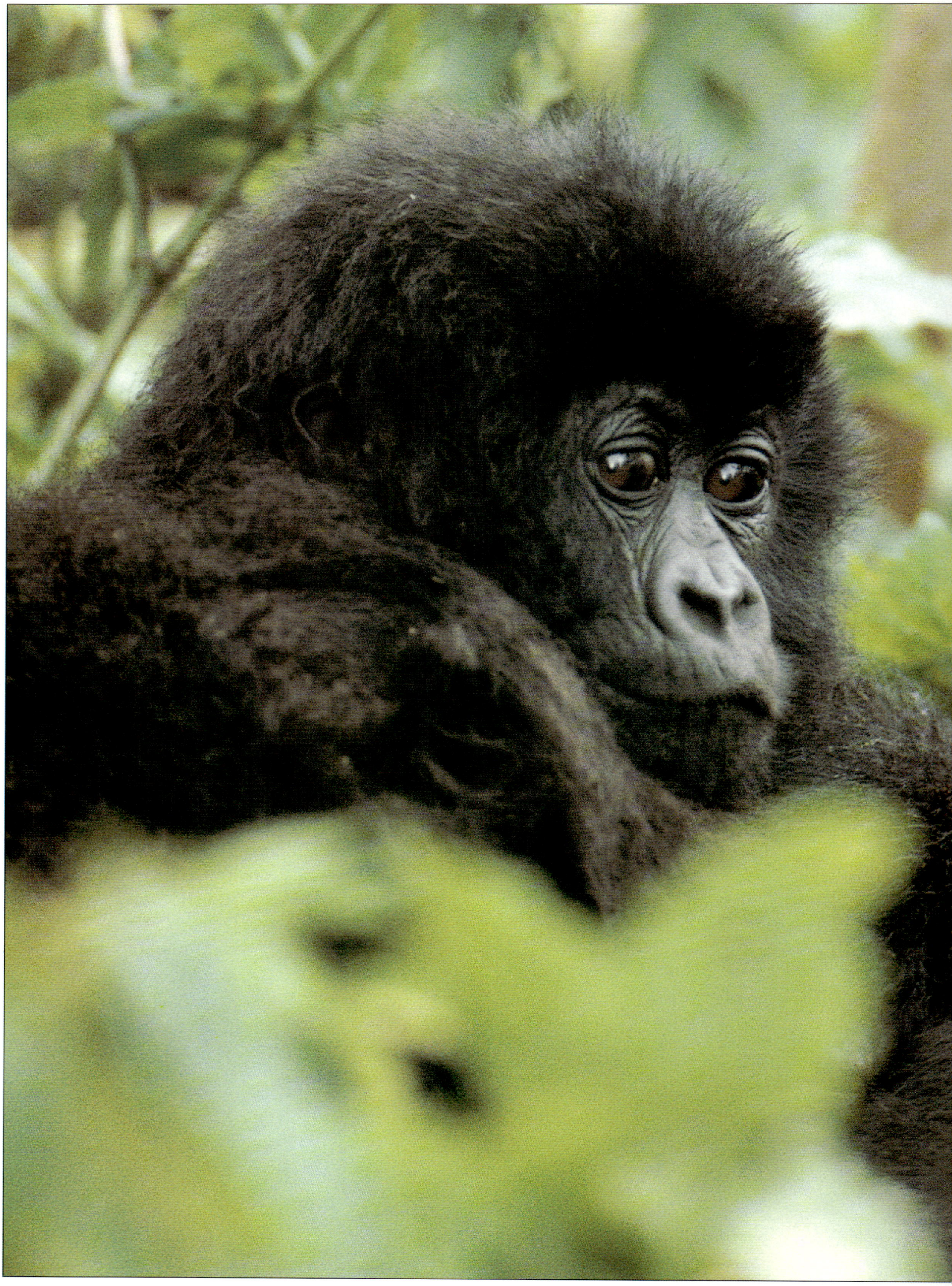

Two youngsters holding on to each other for comfort while viewing the invading tourist groups.

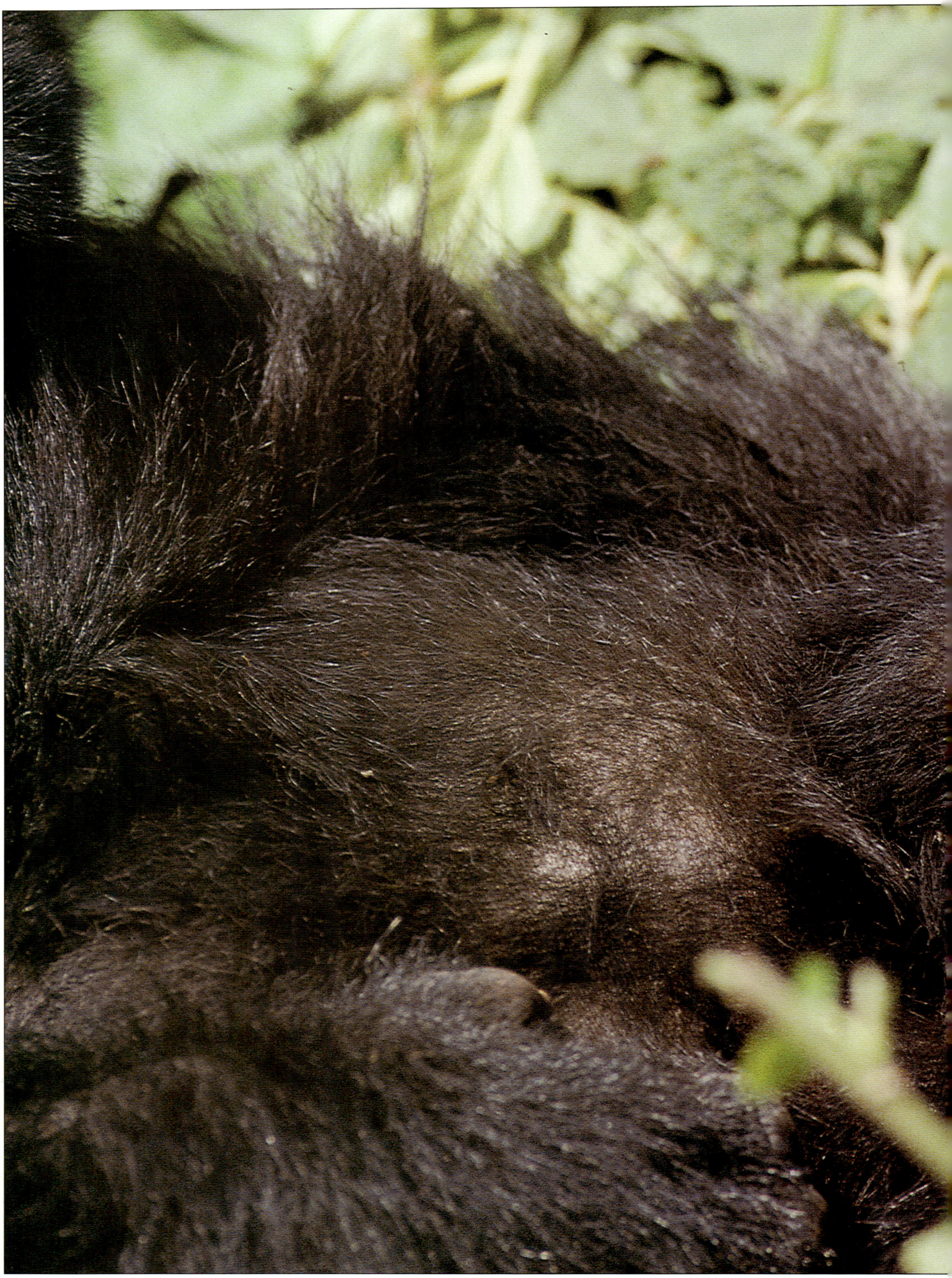

Gorilla play and laughter are actions which are rarely observed.

122

Leaning on a friend for comfort while preparing for a grooming session.

Is that special morsel of food worth the extra effort?

Silverback Naninja in profile. On average, the eastern lowland gorilla is the largest of the three subspecies.

While physical contact is discouraged, John, a park ranger in Kahuzi Biega,

feels that a close relationship helps in the study of the animals.

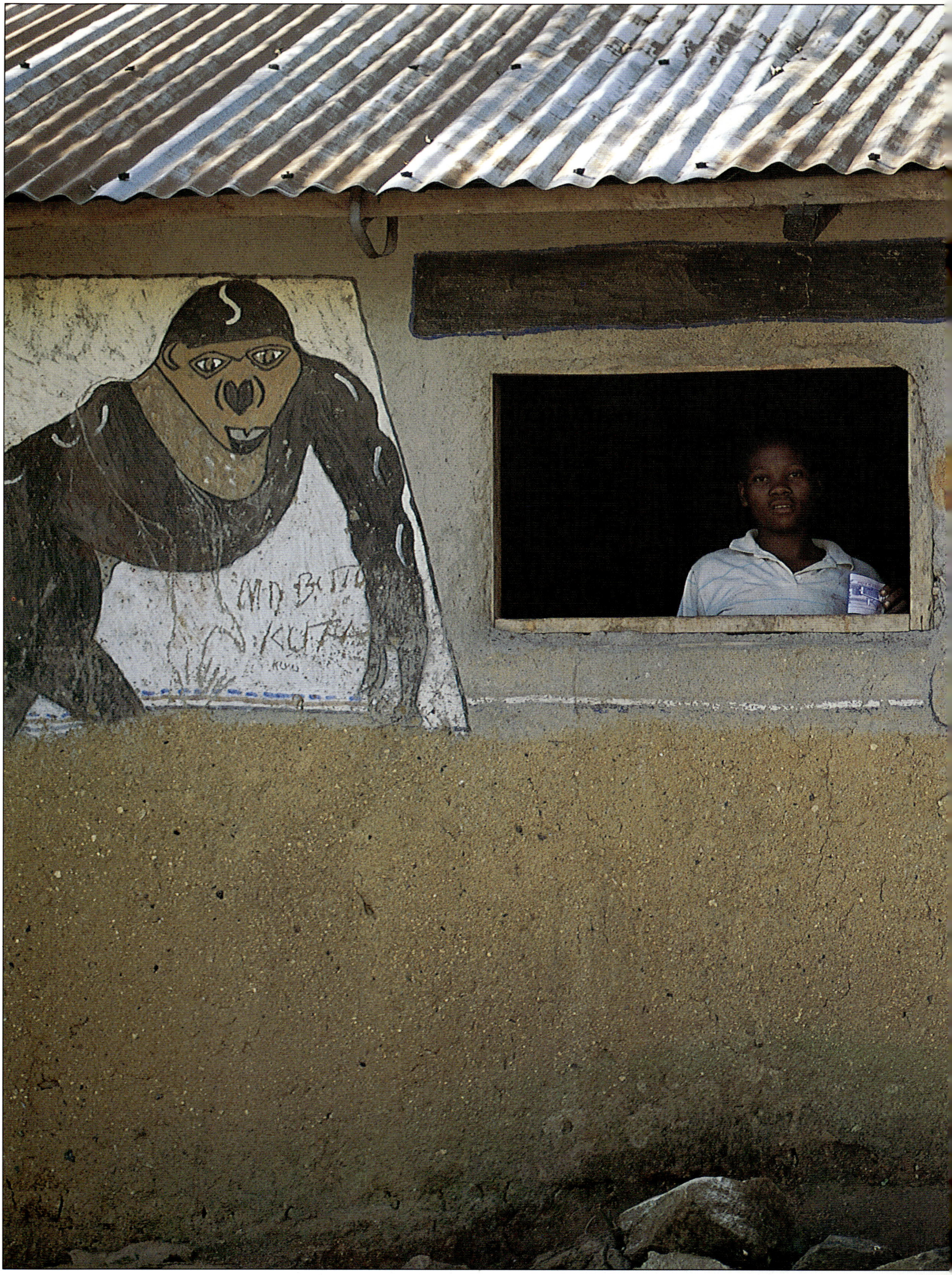

Gorilla graffiti glimpsed on the way to Hombo at the edge of Kahuzi Biega. In this area the gorilla is a familiar sight to the villagers.

The western lowland gorilla is probably the most agile of the three subspecies, frequently climbing trees and feeding on fruit.

The Western Lowland Gorilla

Although the western lowland gorilla (*G.g. gorilla*) is the subspecies most often exhibited in zoos throughout the world, it is also the least studied of the three. There are no habituated groups of western lowland gorillas as they are difficult to reach, living in the deep dark forests of the Congo basin. As this subspecies is frequently hunted, they tend to shy away from human contact and are difficult to approach. Still, recent genetic studies done at Harvard University indicate striking differences in the DNA composition of the western lowland gorilla and the two East African subspecies – the mountain gorilla and the eastern lowland gorilla – making a strong case for the western lowland gorilla to be classified as a separate species altogether. According to Harvard University scientist Maryellen Ruvolo, the genetic differences are even greater than those between the chimpanzee and the bonobo, which are classified as separate species.

With an estimated population of 50–80,000, the number of western lowland gorillas is far larger than the other two subspecies, which probably accounts for the general lack of concern about conservation. Western lowland gorillas are also spread out over a much larger region – the lowland rainforest areas of Cameroon, Central African Republic, Gabon, Congo, Equatorial Guinea, Nigeria and the Cabinda region of Angola. However, western lowland gorillas are not exclusively found in low lying areas; small numbers have been seen up to 1,500m (4,921ft) in the Cross River area of Nigeria and 600m (1,968ft) in parts of Cameroon.

The western lowland subspecies is the smallest of the gorillas, with an average male weighing 140kg (308lbs) and the female 75kg (165lbs). They also tend to live in smaller groups. Also known as the coast gorilla, the western lowland gorilla is characterised by a sagittal crest (the bony ridge on the top of its head) which is moderately high, a wide splayed nose, smaller jaws and teeth, short pelage hair, and a colour that varies widely from black to reddish brown. Often, the western lowland gorilla also has a crest of red or auburn on the head. In the adult male, the silvery grey saddle extends to the rump and thighs. Since western lowland gorillas roam about in dark and dense forests where there is little light, primatologists believe that the larger and more striking saddle of silvery grey hair highlights the presence of the silverback in the territory so that it is readily discernible to the rest of the group. Compared with the mountain gorilla, the western subspecies has a more muscular torso as it roams within a larger territory and climbs trees more frequently. Like its eastern cousin, this subspecies thrives on a diet of mainly foliage and fruit. In fact, research shows that lowland gorillas eat more than a hundred species of plants, a diet more similar to that of the chimpanzee than the mountain gorilla.

In November 1995, I came across a "Kooloo-Kamba" (supposedly a hybrid from a sexual union between a gorilla and a chimpanzee) called Antoine at Yaounde Zoo, Cameroon. A strange looking creature (*see page 143*), Antoine had a short stocky body and a pronounced eyebrow ridge and one canine lodged near the nasal cavity. Although hunters have reported the existence of a third species of great ape, sexual intercourse between a gorilla and a chimp is biologically very unlikely, given the vast differences in genital morphology and sexual behaviour. I provided samples of Antoine's hair to several geneticists. Investigators in Japan have already concluded that Antoine indeed represents a new subspecies or possibly even species of great ape. Alas, he will never know. Antoine has since passed away. Ironically, he may become famous in death after having lived a miserable life in a decrepit zoo.

A lowland bamboo forest. Bamboo is used for a wide range of purposes:

water piping, furniture, roofing and as frames for the typical mud huts.

A reflective village woman, probably contemplating the not-too-rosy economic scenario of Central and West Africa.

The butterfly was probably more at ease than this shy village boy.

The majority of gorillas in captivity in zoos and safari parks around the world belong to the western lowland subspecies.

I found this orphan tied to a post in a Gabonese village. Desperate and dehydrated, she was on the verge of giving up. I delivered her to the Brazzaville gorilla sanctuary in the Congo Republic.

Separated from their families, Brazzaville orphans learn how to feed through trial and error.

In the wild these animals would have their mothers as role models.

Two teenagers on their afternoon outing through the Brazzaville sanctuary.

They have since been relocated to a rehabilitation site in the centre of the country.

It takes a while before sanctuary orphans have the confidence to leave their keepers.

The so-called Kooloo-Kamba (supposed gorilla-chimpanzee hybrid) named Antoine at Yaounde Zoo, Cameroon.

It is possible that this animal could be a new species of the great ape family.

In some regions the mighty Zaire river is the border line for the

distribution of the eastern lowland and western lowland gorillas.

Cameroon alone exports some US$165 million worth of hardwood every year, making it the fifth largest environment; new roads built to transport the logs have

producer of timber in the world. Such unbridled logging has wreaked havoc on the people and the

opened up wildlife-rich forests to commercial hunting.

A young blackback beating his chest despite the loss of his right hand in a snare.

Often such wounds go septic resulting in the animal's death.

A Rwanda government soldier accompanying tourists on a gorilla visit in 1994, at about the time when the rebel army that eventually overthrew the government started their sorties from Uganda.

Saving the Great Apes

The mountain gorilla (*G.g. beringei*) is generally considered the most threatened of the three subspecies as there are only 340 of these creatures left in the world, found in the Virunga volcanoes region which straddles Zaire, Rwanda and Uganda – although scientists still argue whether an additional 320 gorillas in the Bwindi forest in Uganda should be added to the subspecies. For more than a decade, the Mountain Gorilla Project, funded by several eminent conservation organizations, has done an excellent job in keeping the mountain gorilla in the public eye and preventing its precious numbers from being harmed. Recent upheavals in Rwanda, however, have turned the Virunga area into a battle zone with many thousands of refugees and soldiers trampling through the forests and exposing the gorillas to gunfire and disease. To date, eight mountain gorillas have been killed – four in Uganda and four in Zaire (three of whom were shot at point blank range, including the silverback Rugabo who is extensively featured in this book).

Concern is mounting on how to protect the diminishing numbers of mountain gorillas and their habitat. Bolstering the efforts of mountain gorilla conservation groups is the new Rwandan government, which appears to be committed to the protection of the apes, both for favourable international publicity as well as economic reasons. Before the start of the civil war, gorilla tourism was one of Rwanda's main sources of foreign exchange earnings. Naturally, the present government is anxious to revive this source of income. On the Zairian side of the Virungas, however, the future of the mountain gorillas is less secure. Squatter camps now litter the Virunga countryside, holding some 750,000 ethnic Hutu who fled from Rwanda when the rebel forces took over the country in 1994. Fearing reprisals from the new Rwandan government, many are staying put despite the deplorable conditions. Living from hand to mouth, they have turned to the surrounding rainforest to scratch out a living, in the process encroaching on the natural habitat of the mountain gorillas. According to a study made by the United Nations High Commission for Refugees (UNHCR), some 500 to 700 hundred tonnes of wood and grass are removed from the Virunga forests each day, rapidly depleting the habitat of the mountain gorillas.

Mountain gorillas today enjoy a certain celebrity status, thanks to their relatively small numbers and the fact that they have been the subject of countless books, movies and documentaries over the past few decades. Eminent primatologists and scientists like Dian Fossey (whose life was dramatised in the movie *Gorillas in the Mist*) and George Schaller have championed the mountain gorilla conservation cause so effectively that the loss of a single ape today will hog media headlines all over the world. When the silverback Rugabo was shot dead in Zaire in August 1995, the story was immediately picked up by major international publications and television networks around the world; *Time* magazine devoted an entire page to the story and *National Geographic* ran a piece on the dire situation in the Virungas. Sadly the fact that on the same day possibly a dozen members from the western and eastern lowland subspecies were butchered for their meat receives little attention from the world media.

Although the relatively higher numbers of the eastern lowland (3–5,000) and western lowland (50–80,000) gorillas means less cause for alarm, recent studies show that at the current level of attrition, lowland gorillas may face extinction by the end of this century, sharing the fate that their mountain cousins now face. Another subject that often makes media headlines is the smuggling of great ape orphans. However, contrary to popular belief the trade in live animals is no longer a serious threat. Practically all these orphans are a mere by-product of the bush meat trade and their value is often closely linked to that of their weight in terms of fresh meat.

Top: Consumption of bush meat is traditional with the pygmies and some of the Bantu tribes. Bottom: A bush meat market in Pont Noire, Congo. Meat from protected species is easily disguised by smoking and cutting it up into sellable portions.

Bush meat, which refers to any kind of game meat, from antelope and elephants to primates and even snakes, is one of the main sources of protein in the countries of West and Central Africa. In the Congo Republic alone, some 40,000 tons of bush meat are consumed every year. The meat is either sold fresh or smoked as a means of preservation, and is available as whole carcasses or smaller hunks in many village and town markets in the region. This carnage takes place daily, despite the fact that all great apes, from the common chimpanzee to the endangered mountain gorilla, are protected by national wildlife laws governing endangered species and hunting seasons. In the Congo Republic it is estimated that some 600 gorillas and 3,000 chimpanzees end up in the cooking pot every year. While carrying out a survey in southern Cameroon in 1995 I interviewed several dozen hunters and concluded that in an area of some 10,000 sq kms around 800 gorillas are shot annually. Some 25 guns are active in day-time hunting on any given day, and gorillas are taken on about every tenth outing. Allowing a maximum of 0.4 gorillas per sq km, the estimated gorilla population of the area is not likely to exceed 4,000 animals. If these projections are accurate, then the rate of attrition is no longer sustainable and probably has not been for some time.

The consumption of bush meat is a tradition that is deeply entrenched in rural African culture. Why then is a practice that has been going on for decades so suddenly and rapidly depleting the number of primates? The answer lies in the proliferation of the timber trade in Central and West Africa. Foreign and state-owned companies have been logging the forests in the region for some 30 years now, especially in the Congo, Central African Republic (CAR) and Cameroon triangle, which also happens to be one of the last strongholds of the remaining great ape population. Cameroon alone exports US$165 million dollars worth of hardwood each year – with French companies dominating the trade – making it the fifth largest exporter of timber in the world. Plans are to double production by the year 2000.

Research I undertook on behalf of the World Society for the Protection of Animals (WSPA) resulted in a report to the European Parliament which highlighted the relationship between logging and the increasing commercialisation of the bush meat trade. In addition, there are the moral and ecological aspects of degrading one of the last remaining forest tracts in the world and the numerous social and economic repercussions for the local inhabitants. In South America and South-east Asia some tribal groups have started fighting back and received a considerable amount of media attention; the pygmy tribes of Africa are encountering the same conflict scenario without the world hearing about it.

A bush meat seminar sponsored by WSPA in the southern Cameroonian town of Bertoua in 1996 had law enforcement officials going on record stating that many of the new commercial hunters who entered logging concessions were actually fugitives from the law and that the local people were often seeking help to keep these undesirable newcomers out.

Pygmies and other local tribes have hunted for thousands of years, with great apes being occasionally taken. In the past nets, snares, spears and bow-and-arrows were used and subsistence hunting was the order of the day. Logging companies, however, have inadvertently tipped the balance by providing the infrastructure which made the commercialisation of the trade possible. While new roads, bridges and ferries allow timber to be transported from previously inaccessible forest tracts in central Africa to the ocean ports in a matter of days, at the same time they provide commercial hunters with easy access to virgin forest which is still rich in wildlife. Hunting camps spring up wherever logging camps are established. The logging work-force becomes a captive

Top: Many of the drivers of logging trucks transport bush meat. These chimpanzee arms and legs were hidden in the engine compartment of a lorry coming from the Congo. Bottom: Joseph with a silverback carcass in its smoked form.

market for bush meat protein. Quantities shot in excess of local demand are easily exported to town markets. Most lorry drivers supplement their income by trading in bush meat. In addition, there are specialised bush meat traders who use the new logging roads to take their own vehicles to their suppliers in the hunting camps. Other hunters use the logging vehicles to get to the road-head with the first shift in the morning and back to their market in the logging camp later in the same day. Old logging tracks are used to enter the forest and read spoor, from which a good hunter can tell what animal crossed, when, and if it is worthwhile to set a snare or start pursuit.

Joseph is a typical commercial hunter. He arrived in the SEBC logging concession some four years ago. He grew up in the English-speaking part of western Cameroon, where his father told him of gorillas still living near his home village when he was a boy, although he never saw them himself. By the time he was a teenager they were all gone. As an adult Joseph started a life of roaming. For a while he had a job with a western conservation outfit, running programmes at Korrup National Park. From there he went north, smuggling petrol from Nigeria into Cameroon, where he came into conflict with the law. He became a trader, buying goods in the towns and selling or trading them in remote villages. That is how he ended up at 'Bordeaux' village in the SEBC logging concession. The villagers had money, they were already hunting commercially, and Joseph did good business. He decided to stay, and married a local pygmy girl. Today he is one of the main commercial hunters operating out of the village. His double-barrelled 12-guage French-made shotgun is leased from a government official working for the ministry of housing in nearby Batouri to whom he pays a monthly rent of US$20 either in cash or in kind by supplying bush meat. The gun is used most days and nights – night hunting using head-mounted torches can be very productive. Joseph employs another hunter and two pygmy helpers and trackers, and besides the hunting with the gun, he has also staked out a territory in which he operates some 150 snares which he checks every second or third day.

Joseph speaks relatively good English, which is the reason why I have visited him regularly with documentary film crews intent on getting live interviews. When the UK Channel 4 crew first met up with him in 1995 his neighbour had just shot a silverback gorilla which Joseph and his people helped to cut up into manageable portions. Later I visited him again, to find Joseph smoking a female and her baby, which he had shot that day. As is often the case, the infant had been injured by a stray pellet and he had decided to put it down with his machete. In December that year I visited again; this time Joseph had a smoked silverback as well as a young gorilla cut up and ready to be sold to a dealer. In March 1996 we arrived on a Sunday. A dealer had arrived on the previous Friday, and collected among other carcases the meat of a female gorilla and that of a baby. With the weekly supplies being picked up on Fridays, Joseph and his employees generally take the weekend off. And in the run-up to Christmas he spends two consecutive hard weeks in the forest to supply the festive demand, which includes specific orders for gorillas from some of his clients in Bertoua.

Joseph estimates that he and his hunters kill around 50 great apes every year, of which the chimps make up a smaller proportion, because they are more likely to flee than gorillas. Based on what I saw, this estimate does not appear to be an exaggerated figure. Joseph has one major customer, who I shall call Thomas, a dealer who lives in Bertoua. Besides buying meat, he also has guns out on loan to neighbouring hunters and supplies cartridges. Thomas generally arrives on Thursday and departs on Friday. During the rainy season, when hunting is more productive, he will rent a pick-up to collect between one and two tons of meat every week. During the dry season he tends to hike lifts on the SEBC logging lorries. Thomas holds an official licence to deal in bush meat. It

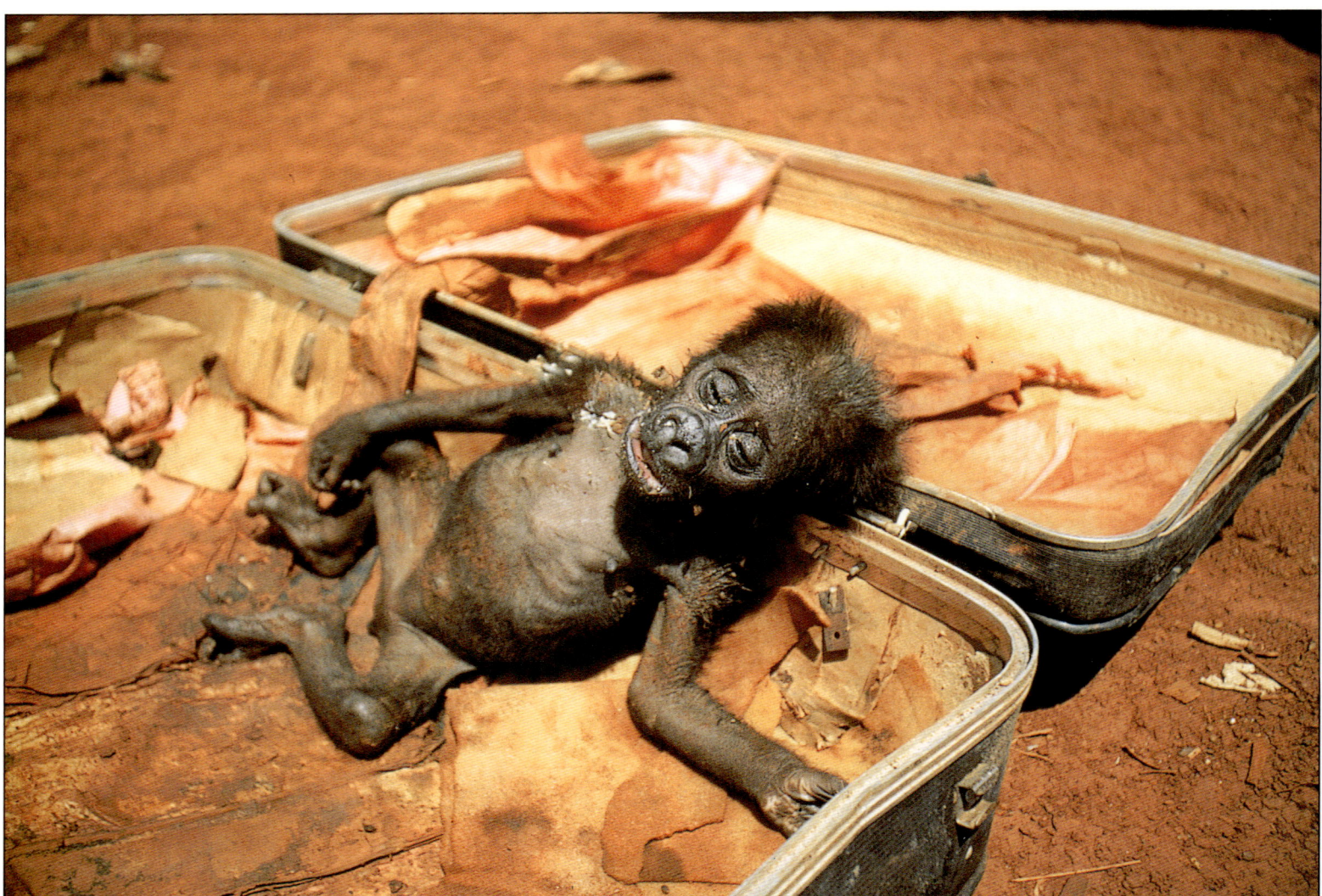

Top: This gorilla was shot on request for a police chief. For his services, the hunter was allowed to retain the head and an arm.

Bottom: The body of an orphaned baby gorilla in the suitcase where it died.

stipulates that he pay a tax of CFA200 for each small carcass, and the same amount for cuts of a bigger animal – although it gives no indication what animals are included and which are protected. When he showed us his licence in December 1995 it had expired the previous October, and someone had re-validated it with a signature and a stamp. Thomas also supplies Joseph with cartridges. They are normally issued against a licence which gives the corresponding hunting and gun licence numbers. Joseph has no licence at all, but Thomas sells him whatever cartridges he needs, no questions asked. If elephants are spotted in the area, there is a high-powered rifle available for rent in a neighbouring village. Thomas will supply the corresponding bullets as well. Eleven elephants were killed with this particular gun in 1995.

'Bordeaux' village also has an official bush meat shop, whose main customers are logging lorry drivers. At the door is a hand-written price list for different cuts of fresh and smoked meat. The document is stamped and signed by the village chief. When I asked the dealer why he had not listed elephant and gorilla meat, he told me that it was illegal to sell it openly. However, he had a supply of both, if I was interested. He also offered raw ivory and had two skulls of very small elephants used as ashtrays in the shop.

Joseph is thinking of relocating because of diminishing yields in his region. Not far from his camp another concession-holder has started a new logging road which will link 'Bordeaux' directly to Lomie, some 30 kms (19 miles) away. A considerable amount of traffic goes from there to Yaounde, the capital. This move will allow Joseph to exploit new hunting grounds as well as reach new customers. Thus a domino effect of new roads and camps leads to the systematic hunting of gorilla and chimp groups.

Joseph considers himself to be an expert in gorilla behaviour. He classifies them as stupid, because while chimps will flee, gorillas stand their ground, and get shot. He illustrates how quickly he can load his double-barrelled gun; by shooting a female first he will almost certainly be charged by the silverback, and he will be ready for the male with two buckshot cartridges. Sometimes such a charge is followed by a young blackback joining the older male, and Joseph states that on two occasions he took four gorillas in one go using this technique.

Apart from the commercialization of bush meat, indiscriminate hunting of chimps and gorillas has resulted in hundreds of orphaned apes. The hunters' main objective is to secure the largest possible chunk of protein, and having tracked down a gorilla or chimp family, they will generally go for the animal that represents the easiest target i.e. the adult animals protecting the young. In the case of the gorilla, however, the hunters will try to take the male silverback first, since he is likely to charge if a member of his family is under threat. If the baby animals survive and are not wounded by stray shotgun pellets, the hunters bring them back to the villages where they often end up as playthings for the children until they succumb to malnutrition and disease. Most orphans die quietly, tied to some village hut before they ever reach a market. Others are taken to large towns, where the hunters hope to find buyers. In Yokadouma, one such town, I talked to the representative of the ministry of the environment in charge of licensing. He informed me that his policy for dealing with orphans was to return them to the forest where they came from, meaning any such animal confiscated or given to his department would be dropped in a piece of bush somewhere outside town, condemning it to certain death. A very small percentage may still be exported, mostly on Eastern European ships, from such ports as Pointe Noire in the Congo and Conakry in Guinea. The number of animals smuggled out of the country however is minuscule; smuggling endangered species such as gorillas and chimpanzees has become very difficult and risky and thanks to international laws, private animal collectors and medical laboratories would today find

Top: A gorilla orphan serving as a toy in a Gabonese village. Bottom: gorilla hands for sale in a Brazzaville fetish market.

it very hard to explain the origins of such a high profile animal as a gorilla. An additional by-product of the bush meat trade is the use of gorilla body parts as fetishes and in black magic. A dozen stalls in Brazzaville's Ounze market offer such grisly items as gorilla hands and feet, most of which have digits missing. The digits are sold separately, pulverised and sprinkled onto skin abrasions specially inflicted for the purpose, or into the baby's bath in the hope of endowing the child with gorilla-like strength. Joseph has been feeding his young son with gorilla meat for this very objective.

In 1994, I teamed up with the WSPA to organize a campaign to create awareness in the West and hopefully raise funds to launch conservation projects targeting the bush meat trade and help set up orphanages to care for captive apes. Most established conservation organizations consider the issue a complex one, and because of the third-world context, also very culturally sensitive; after all, who are we to tell Africans that they should be more concerned about protecting animals, as long as starvation is still an issue in most of the countries concerned. The fault in this argument is that bush meat is a luxury commodity. In the main towns it is twice as expensive as beef or pork, which is often classified as "white man's meat", and lacking in taste. It is not Africa's poor who consume bush meat. The problem seems to be that the increase in supply has stimulated demand amongst the affluent sections of society. In purely economic terms, it would appear that 2–3,000 hard-core commercial hunters like Joseph do most harm, and reintroducing the closed hunting season and enforcing the laws concerning protected species would somewhat affect their income. As for the rest, nobody would go starving – not the dealers and not the consumers. Thus the economic argument cannot be accepted as an excuse and a reason to look the other way.

Then there is the argument that the economic benefits of logging for most of the third world countries far outweigh the negative environmental impact. Ironically, very little of any logging income seems to go back to the rural areas. Most logging concerns are foreign-owned conglomerates who remove thousands of tons of valuable hardwood each year, with virtually none of the corresponding tax income going back to counteract the local ecological and social impact. In 1995 we interviewed a prominent French logging company executive, who broke rank with his colleagues by going on record as stating that adhering to local laws and regulations would be madness as far as profitability was concerned. As for the bush meat trade, he called it "total destruction" estimating that within 10 to 20 years all the large mammals would have been wiped out in and near the main logging tracts. He cited Liberia, Sierra Leone and the Ivory Coast as examples of what the central African rainforest basin will look like in a decade or two if the present trend continues. He does not think that the loggers or the governments concerned have the know-how or the will to take effective measures. He feels that only an international outcry can force the issue to become a national priority.

And finally, there is the moral issue of consuming creatures whose DNA so closely resembles that of humans. Analysis shows that the genetic code of chimps and gorillas is 98.6 and 97.7 percent human. I keep advancing an argument which is not considered to be very culturally sensitive: cannibalism, especially among the Fang people of Gabon and Cameroon was only eradicated with the arrival of the colonial powers and the missionaries. If it is a question of being culturally sensitive, who is to decide where we draw the line. We do not eat retarded humans. Maybe what Africa needs is an influx of eco-missionaries, working at grass-roots levels, wiping out what I consider to be 98.6 and 97.7 cannibalism. If we find no solution to keeping our closest ancestors in the animal kingdom out of the cooking pot, what hope is there for other species, and for the future of mankind itself?

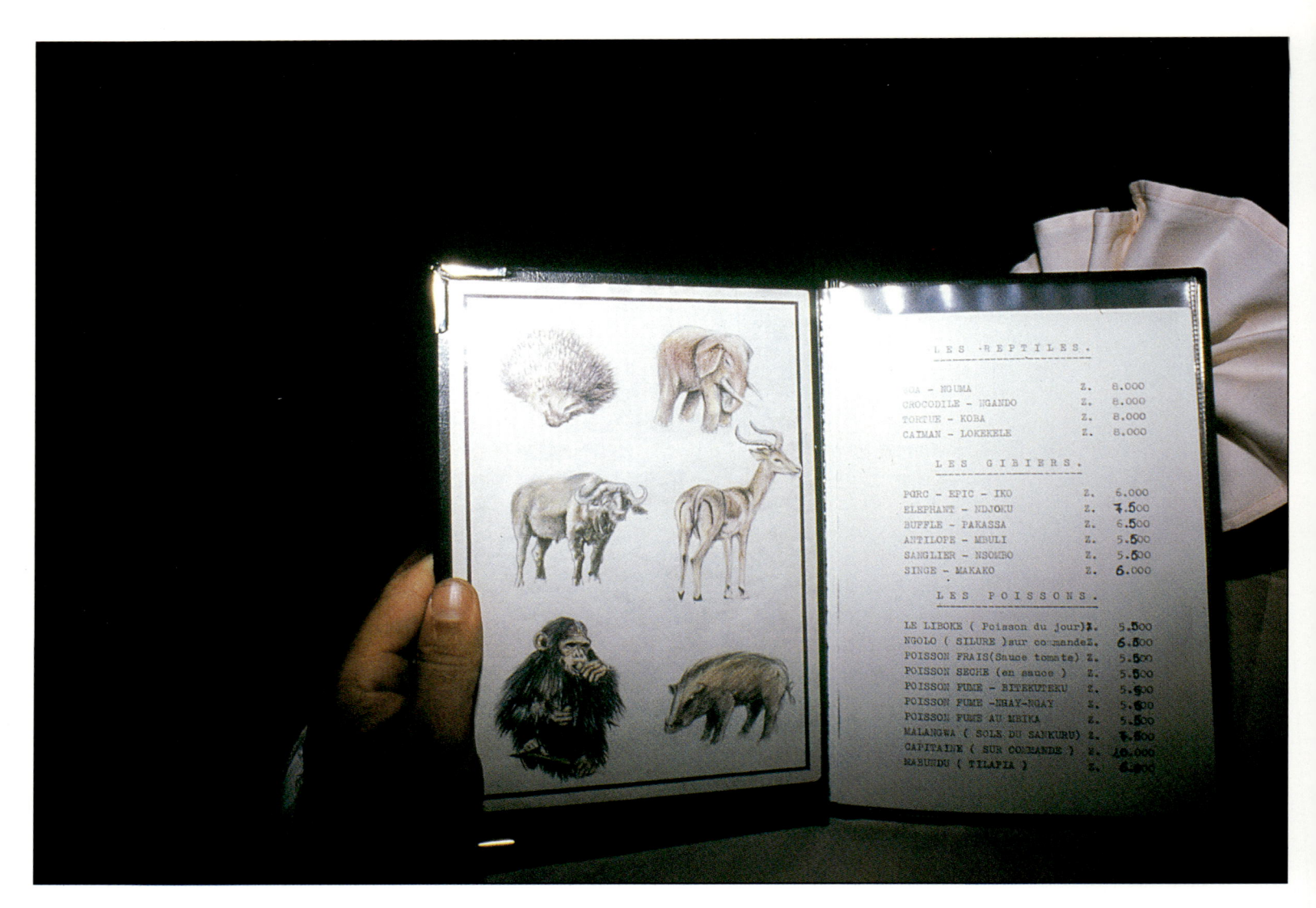

Top: Disregard of local law – such as treating endangered species as menu items – has to be controlled.

Bottom: Traditional village life has been replaced by a culture of commercial hunting, turning the next generation into potential poachers.

Conservation Recommendations

During the Bush Meat Conference held in Bertoua, Cameroon, in April 1995, several resolutions were passed which could represent a blueprint for other nations with similar problems to tackle. They included:

- A programme to educate people on the necessity of preserving the biodiversity of the ecosystem in general and of endangered species in particular.
- Strict implementation of local conservation laws and regulations; empowering local authorities to confiscate poaching equipment and animal carcasses hunted illegally.
- Strengthening regional cooperation between countries, especially in the area of trade and the circulation of cartridges.
- Periodical evaluation of conservation laws and agreements with logging concessions. In addition, governments should exert pressure on logging companies to honour the terms and conditions of their contracts. Errant companies will have their permits withdrawn.
- Proposal of national conservation initiatives seeking the cooperation of governments, foreign wildlife protection agencies and NGOs.
- Raising of funds worldwide to support local conservation programmes.

Actions

- Creation of road check-points specifically to control the bush meat trade.
- Transformation of abandoned logging tracts into controlled hunting zones.
- Closing roads no longer active for logging.
- Ban on the logging of specific trees which contribute to the diet of gorillas and chimps.
- Ban on settlement of local people in active and abandoned logging settlements, based on existing zoning laws.
- Developing alternative income sources for people around logging concessions such as eco-tourism and farming.
- Restricting illegal import of cartridges. Tighter control on local production and distribution of ammunition.
- Bush meat regulations must be part of the certification process for sustainably-logged and exported timber.
- Introduction of grass-root pilot projects to regulate and monitor the bush meat trade.

Any reader interested in helping in programmes and projects which will hopefully result in the implementation of these resolutions should contact:

World Society of Protection of Animals
2 Langley Lane, London SW8 1TJ
Tel: (44) 171 793 0540   Fax: (44) 171 793 0208

Orphaned gorillas at the Brazzaville sanctuary in their night cage.

These two teenagers have since been re-introduced into the wild.